Computer in Education

Computer in Education

Editor

Atul Jain

Computer in Education

ISBN: 81-8205-168-1

Published in 2009 in India by
ISHA Books
B-63, 1st Floor, New Gupta Colony,
Near DDA Market,
Delhi-110009
Phone: 9212142040
ishabooks@hotmail.com

Laser Type Setting by: Shree Vaishnavi Creations, Delhi
Printed at: Vishal Kaushik Printers, Delhi

PREFACE

Since the 1970s, computers have been inserted into schools with much fanfare and great expense. Almost all of the attention to computers has revolved around the question of how to put them to use as tools for education. Subsequent assessments have focused primarily on their effectiveness as an aid to learning and how well students are prepared for their use beyond school. Through all of this, almost no attention has been paid to the more fundamental issue of the effects that the very use of computers has on young people. A determination of the proper role of computers in education must begin with an understanding of the computer's effects on the user.

The various uses of computers in education may be classified into four broad categories. The first one makes use of computer programming as a developmental or authoring tool. The second form of using computers in education is programmed instruction. The third form of computer use in education is simulating experiments. Finally, one may use computers as productivity tools, both within content areas and as an area of study for future use.

The use of the internet for education deserves special mention. It is the newest and thus, as is typical in the world of educational computing, it is being promoted by many as the most powerful tool for learning ever invented. What makes it so powerful is that it allows the child or young person to freely search for educational material or useful information, as well as doing communication with all sorts of people in different parts of the planet. According to this view, the internet provides for a constructivist environment, where the child or young person learns by doing.

Besides their numberless application in education, internet presents a number of complex risks for children who them. The risks include exposure to inappropriate material; physical molestation; harassment; legal and financial issues. Because of these challenges the teacher/parents should supervise children's computer use for the fruitful educational achievements.

The present book is a thoughtful work which provides rich knowledge both about computers and about the process of computer-aided learning. It shows how computers can enhance student motivation and engagement. Readers will learn from the book about the variety of computer software available for teaching. The application of internet in education and the importance of safe use of it are also analysed. Teachers, students, educators and policy makers will be the primary audience of this book.

Editor

CONTENTS

1

INTRODUCTION TO COMPUTERS

HISTORY OF COMPUTERS

When the human race started doing some trade, it felt a need for a calculating device. The first calculating device, which was used 2000 years ago was called *abacus* and the improvements in the calculating device in that age were slow. The next change came after about 1600 years. Following this, the changes were frequent and the mechanical desk calculator was developed around 1800 A.D.

In 1833, Prof. Charles Babbage, the father of the computer, developed a machine called *analytical engine* which was the vase for the modern digital computer.

GENERATION OF COMPUTERS

The electronic digital computers, which were introduced in 1950's, were using *vacuum tubes*. Following this, the development in the electronic components helped in the developed of digital computers also. The second-generation computers used *transistors*.

The introduction of integrated circuits (ICs), also know as chips opened the door for the developed of third generation computers. A very large number of circuit elements (transistors, diodes, resistors, etc.,) could be integrated into a very small (less than 5mm square) surface of silicon and hence the name IC. The third generation computers used *small-scale integrated circuits (SSI)* which contain about 10-20 components. When *large-scale integrated circuits (LSI)* (around 30,000 components) were developed, the fourth generation computers were produced.

DEFINITION OF A COMPUTER

A computer is an electronic device capable of executing instructions, developed based on algorithms stored in its memory, to process data fed to it and produced the required results faster than human beings.

BASIC CONCEPTS

— In order to solve a problem using a computer, it is necessary to find and write an algorithm for it.

— An *algorithm* is a finite sequence of instructions. Each instruction should be precise, unambiguous, and capable of being carried out by a machine in a finite time.

— An algorithm can be expressed in a graphical form know as a *flow chart*.

— A *programming language* is a precise notation used to express algorithms.

— An algorithm expressed in a programming language is called a *computer program*

BASIC UNITS

A computer is designed using four basic units. They are:

1) *Input Unit:* Computers need to receive data and instructions in order to solve any problem. Therefore we need to put the data and instructions into the computer. The input unit consists of one or more input device. The keyboard and

mouse of a computer are the most commonly used input devices.

2) *Central Processing Unit (CPU):* It is the main part of a computer system like the heart of a human being. It interprets the instructions in the program and executes one by one. It consists of three major units.

   — *Control Unit:* It controls and directs the transfer of program instructions and data between various units.

   — *Arithmetic and Logic Unit (ALU):* Arithmetic operations like (+,-,*,^,/), logical operations like (AND, OR, NOT) and relational operations like (<,>,<=,>=) are being carried out in this Unit.

   — *Registers:* They are used to store instructions and data for further use.

3) *Memory Unit:* It is used to store the Programs and data.

4) *Output Unit:* It is used to print/display the results, which are stored in the memory unit.

Secondary stored devices refer to floppy disks, magnetic disks, magnetic disks, magnetic tapes, hard disks, compact disks etc., which are used to store huge information for future use. The input unit, output unit and secondary storage devices are together know as Peripheral devices.

The block diagram of a computer is shown in the next page.

The components of a computer are connected by using buses. A bus is a collection of wire that carry electronic signals from one component to another. There are standard buses such as Industry Standard Architecture (ISA), Extended Industry Standard Architecture (EISA), Micro-Channel Architecture (MCA), and so on. The standard bus permits the user to purchase the components from different vendors and connect them easily.

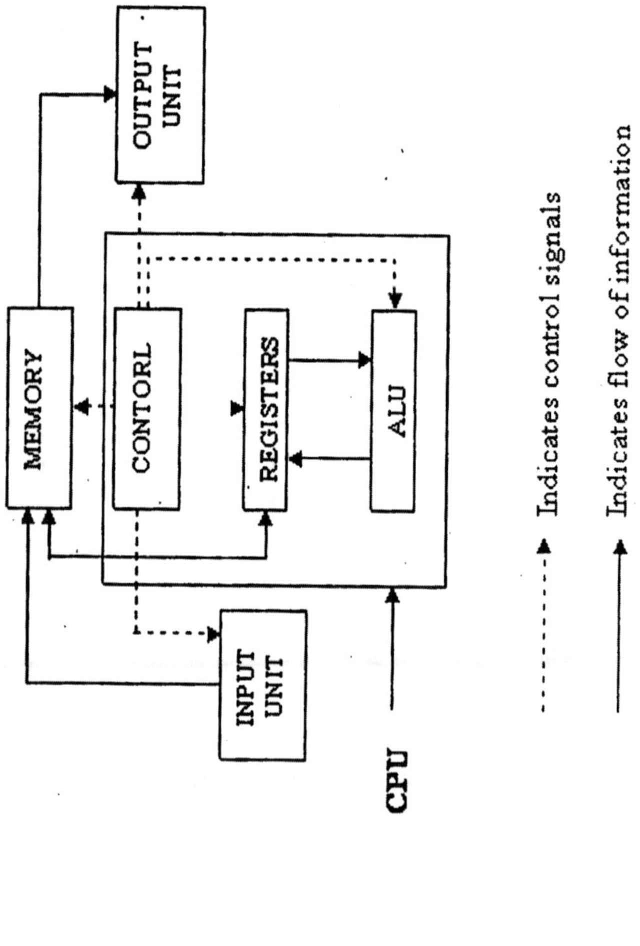

Figure 1. Block diagram of a computer

The various input and output devices have a standard way of connecting to the CPU and Memory. These are called interface standards. Some popular interface standards are the RS-232C and Small Computer System Interconnect (SCSI). The places where the standard interfaces are provided are called ports.

DATA REPRESENTATION

Bits and Bytes

Data in Computers are represented using only two symbols '0' & '1'. These are called " Binary digiTS" (or) "*BITS*" for short. A set of 8 bits is called a *byte* and each byte stores one character. 2n Unique strings are represented using n bits only. For example, Using 2 bits we can represent 4=(22) unique strings as 00, 01, 10, 11. ASCII (American Standards Code for Information Interchange) codes are used to represent each character. The ASCII code includes codes for English Letters (Both Capital & Small), decimal digits, 32 special characters and codes for a number of symbols used to control the operation of a computer which are non-printable.

Binary numbers

Binary numbers are formed using the positional notation. Powers of 2 are used as weights in the binary number system. A binary number system. A binary number 10111, has a decimal value equal to 1*24+0*23+1*21+1*20=23. A decimal number is converted into an equivalent binary number by dividing the number by 2 and storing the remainder as the least significant bit of the binary number. For example, consider the decimal number 23. Its equivalent binary number is obtained as show in figure 2.

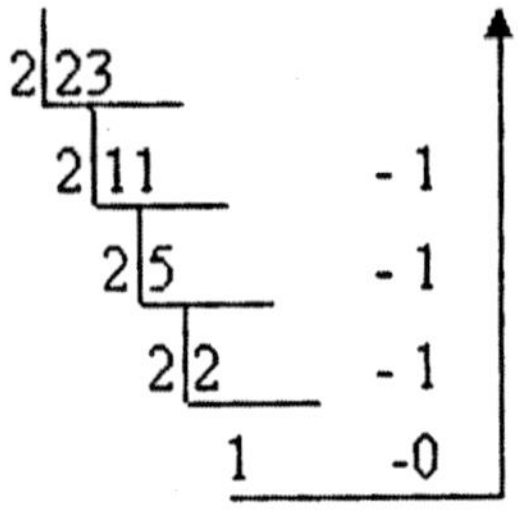

Figure 2. Conversion of Decimal to Binary Example.23. = 10111^2

Hexadecimal Numbers

High valued binary numbers will be represented by a long sequence of 0's and 1's. A more concise representation is using hexadecimal representation. The base of the hexadecimal system is 16 and the symbols used in this system are 0,1,2,4,5,6,7,8,9,A,B,C,D,E,F. Strings of 4 bits have an equivalent hexadecimal value. For example, *6B* is represented by 0110 1011 or 110 1011, *3E1* is represented by 0011 1110 0001 or 11 1110 0001 and *5DBE34* is represented by 101 1101 1011 1110 0011 0100. Decimal fractions can also be converted to binary fractions.

Parity Check Bit

Errors may occur while recording and reading data and when data is transmitted from one unit to another unit in a computer Detection of a single error in the code for a character is possible by introducing an extra bit in its code. This bit, know as the *parity check bit*, is appended to the code. The user can set the parity bit either as even or odd. the user chooses this bit so that the total number of ones ('1') in the new code is *even* or *odd* depending upon the selection. If a single byte is incorrectly read or written or transmitted, then the error can be identified using the parity check bit.

HARDWARE

The *hardware* are the parts of computer itself including the *Central Processing Unit (CPU)* and related *microchips* and *micro-circuitry*, *keyboards*, *monitors*, *case* and *drives* (floppy, hard, CD, DVD, optical, tape, etc...). Other extra parts called *peripheral components* or *devices* include *mouse*, *printers*, *modems*, *scanners*, *digital cameras* and *cards* (*sound*, *colour*, *video*) etc... Together they are often referred to as a *personal computers* or *PCs*.

Central Processing Unit (CPU)

Though the term relates to a specific chip or the *processor* a CPU's performance is determined by the the rest of the computers *circuitry* and *chips*.

A processing unit in a computer interprets instructions in a program and carries them out. An instruction in general, consists of a part, which specifies the them out. An instruction in general, consist of a part, which specifies the operation to be performed and other parts, which specify the address of operand. In a processor, a strong of bits is used to code operations and another string of n operations in binary so that 2x = n. For example to code 16 operations we need 4 bits, since 24=16.

An instruction consisting of an operation code and operand address or addresses designed for a specific computer is know as a machine language instruction of that computer. Machine language instructions for input/output, data movement, arithmetic, logic and controlling sequence of operations are available in all computers. A computer's processor has storage registers to store operands and results. It also has a register to store the instruction being executed called "Instruction Register" and a register which store the address of the next instruction to be executed called " Program Counter Register"

A sequence of machine language instructions to solve a problem is know as a machine language program. A computer executes a machine language programs in two phases. In the first phase, it reads and stores the program in its memory. After storing the program, it initiates program execution. In this phase, instructions are retrieved from memory one after another and are decoded and executed.

Currently the Pentium chip or processor, made by Intel, is the most common CPU though there are many other companies that produce processors for personal computers. One example is the CPU made by Motorola which is used in Apple computers.

Figure 3. Chip

With faster processors the *clock speed* becomes more important. Compared to some of the first computers which operated at below 30 *megahertz* (MHz) the Pentium chips began at 75 MHz in the late 1990's. As of mid 2003 speeds now exceed 3000+ MHz or 3 *gigahertz* (GHz) (check your local computer store for the latest speed). It depends on the *circuit board* that the chip is housed in, or the *motherboard*, as to whether you are able to upgrade to a faster chip. The motherboard contains the circuitry and connections that allow the various component to communicate with each other.

Though there were many computers using many different processors previous to this were the 80286 processors. The advent of home computers as these were the processors that made computers available for the average person. Using a processor before the 286 involved learning a proprietary system and software. Most new software are being developed for the newest and fastest processors so it can be difficult to use an older computer system.

Keyboard

The keyboard is used to type information into the computer or *input* information. There are many different keyboard layouts and sizes with the most common for Latin based languages being the QWERTY layout (named for the first 6 keys). The standard keyboard has 101 keys. Notebooks have embedded keys accessible by *special* keys or by pressing key combinations (CTRL or Command and P for example). *Ergonomically* designed keyboards are designed to make typing easier.

Some of the keys have a special use. There are referred to as *command keys.* The 3 most common are the Control or CTRL, Alternate or Alt and the Shift keys though there can be more (the Windows key for example or the Command key). Each key on a standard keyboard has one or two *characters.* Press the key to get the lower character and hold Shift to get the upper.

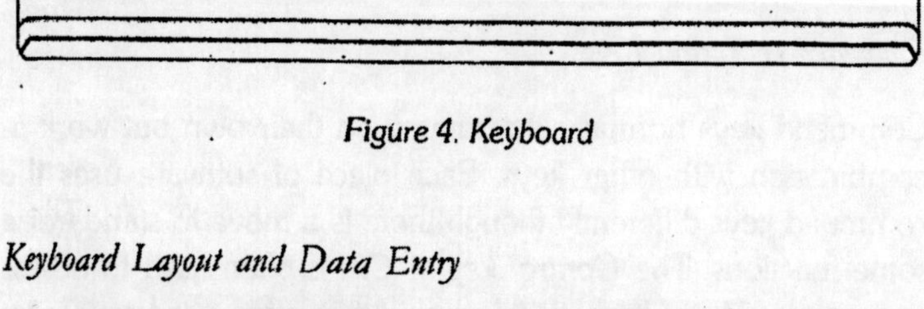

Figure 4. Keyboard

Keyboard Layout and Data Entry

— *ENTER* or *RETURN* - Moves the cursor down one line and to the left margin. Enter also process commands such as choosing an option in a dialog (message) boxes and submitting a form.

— *DEL* or *DELETE* - Deletes the character at cursor and/or characters to the right of the cursor and all highlighted (or selected) text.

— *BKSP* or *BACKSPACE* - Deletes the character to the left of cursor and all hightlighted text.

— *SPACE BAR* - Moves the cursor one space at a time to the right

— *SHIFT KEY* - Use the shift keys to type capital letters and to type the upper character on keys with two characters on them

— *CAPS LOCK* - Locks the keyboard so it types capital letters (a light goes on when caps lock is on)

— *TAB* - Moves the cursor five spaces to the right (number of spaces are usually adjustable). Tab moves to the next field in a form or table (Shift-Tab for previous field).

— *ESC* or *ESCAPE* - Cancels a menu or dialog box

— *ARROW KEYS* - Moves the cursor around document without changing text

— *FUNCTION KEYS* or *F KEYS* - Access commands by themselves or in combination with the three *command* keys; CTRL, SHIFT, and ALT

Command or Special Keys

Command keys normally do nothing on their own but work in combination with other keys. Each piece of software uses the command keys differently though there is a move to standardize some functions. The *Control key* or *Ctrl* is often used to access commands. The *Alternative key* or *Alt* is often used to access menus. The *Shift key* is used to type CAPITAL LETTERS. As well the command keys are all used to move through documents and edit text faster and easier. As well many computers have *Special keys* design specifically for the particular computer. Apple computers have the *Apple keys* and Macs have *Command keys.* Many keyboards now have a *Windows key* specifically for Windows 9x and newer systems. Many older computers also have special keys used for a variety of different functions.

Some *Notebook* or *Laptop keys* are left out because of space limitations and they usually have a *Special function key* which allows other keys to double for the missing ones.

Mouse

Mouse is a small device held in hand and pushed along a flat surface. It can move the cursor in any direction. In a mouse a small ball is kept inside and the ball touches the pad through a hole at the bottom of the mouse. When the mouse is moved, the ball rolls. This movement of the ball is converted into electronic signals and sent to the computer. Mouse is very popular in the modern computers that use Windows and other Graphical User Interface (GUI) applications.

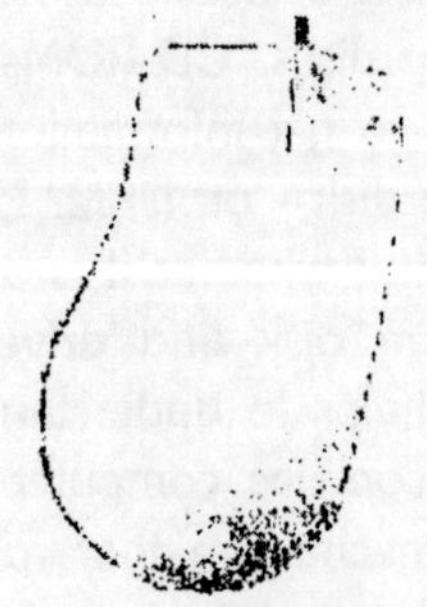

Figure 5. Mouse

Most modern computers today are run using a mouse controlled pointer. Generally if the mouse has two buttons the left one is used to *select* objects and text and the right one is used to *access menus*. If the mouse has one button (Mac for instance) it controls all the activity and a mouse with a third buttons can be used by specific software programs. One type of mouse has a round ball under the bottom of the mouse that rolls and turns two wheels which control the direction of the pointer on the screen. Another type of mouse uses an optical system to track the movement of the mouse.

It is important to clean the mouse periodically, particularly if it becomes sluggish. A ball type mouse has a small circular panel that can be opened, allowing you to remove the ball. Lint can be remove carefully with a tooth pick or tweezers and the ball can be washed with mild detergent. A build up will accumulate on the small wheels in the mouse. Use a small instrument or finger nail to scrap it off taking care not to scratch the wheels. Track balls can be cleaned much like a mouse and touch-pad can be wiped with a clean, damp cloth. An optical mouse can accumulate material from the surface that it is in contact with which can be removed with a finger nail or small instrument.

Disk Drives

Magnetic surface recording devices commonly used in computers are Hard disks, Floppy disks, CD-ROMs and Magnetic tapes. All *disks* need a *drive* to get information off - or *read* - and put information on the disk - or *write*. Each drive is designed for a specific type of disk whether it is a CD, DVD, hard disk or floppy. Often the term 'disk' and 'drive' are used to describe the same thing but it helps to understand that the disk is the *storage device* which contains computer files - or *software* - and the drive is the mechanism that runs the disk. Detailsof the disk devices are discribed below.

Floppy Disk Drive (FDD)

In this device, the medium used to record the data is called as floppy disk. It is a flexible circular disk of diameter 3.5 inches made of plastic coated with a magnetic material. This is housed in a square plastic jacket. Each floppy disk can store approximately on million characters. Data recorded on a floppy disk is read and stored in a computer's memory by a device called a floppy disk is read and stored in a computer's memory by a device called a floppy disk drive (FDD).

A floppy disk is inserted in a slot of the FDD. The disk is rotated normally at 300 revolutions per minute. A reading head is positioned touching a track. A voltage is induced in a coil wound on the head when a magnetized spot moves below the head. The polarity of the induced voltage when a 0 is read. The voltage sensed by the head coil is amplified, converted to an appropriate signal and stored in computer's memory.

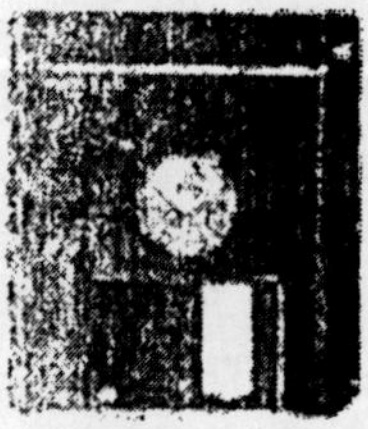

Figure 6. Floppy Disks

Floppy Disks com with various capacities as mentioned below.

— 51/4 drive- 360KB, 1.2MB (1 KB= 210 = 1024 bytes)

— 31/2 drive- 1.44 Mb, 2.88 MB (1MB= 220 bytes)

Compact Disk Drive (CDD)

CD-ROM (Compact Disk Read Only Memory) used a laser beam to record and read data along spiral tracks on a 51/4 disk. A disk can store around 650 MB of information. CD-ROMs are normally used to store massive text data. (such as encyclopedias) which is permanently recorded and read many times. Recently CD writers have come in the market. Using a

CD writer, lot of information can be written on CD-ROM and stored for future reference.

Figure 7. Compact Disk Drive (CDD)

Hard Disk Drive (HDD)

Unlike a floppy disk that is flexible and removable, the hard disk used in the PC is permanently fixed. The hard disk used in a higher end Pc can have a maximum storage capacity of 17 GB (Giga Byte; 1 GB= 1024 MB = 230 bytes). Now a days, hard disks capacities of 540 MB, 1 GB, 2 GB, 4 GB and 8 GB are quite common. The data transfer rate between the CPU and hard disk is much higher as compared to the between the CPU and the floppy disk drive.

The CPU can use the hard disk to load programs and data as well as to store data. The hard disk is a very important Input/Output (I/O) device. The hard disk drive doesn't require any special care other than the requirement that one should operate the PC within a dust-free and cool room (preferably air-conditioned).

In summary, a computer system is organized with a balanced configuration of different types of memories. The main memory (RAM) is used to store program being currently executed by the computer. Disks are used to store large data files and program files. Tapes are serial access memories and used to backup the files form the disk. CD-ROMs are used to store user manuals, large text, audio and video data.

Monitors

Monitors provide a visual display of data. It looks like a television. It shows information on the screen when you type. This is called *outputting* information. When the computer needs more information it will display a message on the screen, usually through a *dialog box*. Monitors come in many types and sizes from the simple monochrome (one colour) screen to full colour screens.

Most desktop computers use a monitor with a *cathode tube* and most notebooks use a *liquid crystal display* (LCD) monitor.

To get the full benefit of today's software with full colour graphics and animation, computers need a color monitor with a display or *graphics card*.

Monitors are of different types and have different display capabilities. These capabilities are determined by a special circuit called the Adapter card. Some popular adapter cards are,

— Color Graphics Adapter (CGA)

— Enhanced Graphics Adapter (EGA)

— Video Graphics Array (VGA)

— Super Video Graphics Array (SVGA)

The smallest dot that can be displayed is called a pixel. The number of pixels that can be displayed vertically and horizontally gives the maximum resolution of the monitor. The resolution of the monitor determines the quality of the display. The higher the resolution the better is the quality of the display. Some popular resolution are 800*640 pixels, 1024*768 pixels, 1280*1024 pixels.

Printers

The printer takes the information on your screen and transfers it to paper or a *hard copy*. There are many different types of printers with various levels of quality. The three basic types of printer are; *dot matrix*, *inkjet*, and *laser*.

— Dot matrix printers work like a typewriter transferring ink from a ribbon to paper with a series or 'matrix' of tiny pins.

— Ink jet printers work like dot matrix printers but fires a stream of ink from a cartridge directly onto the paper.

— Laser printers use the same technology as a photocopier using heat to transfer toner onto paper.

Line printer

It prints a complete line at a time. Printing speed varies from 150 lines to 2500 lines per minute with 96 to 160 character on a 15-inch line. Six to eight lines per vertical inch are printed. Usually 64 and 96 character sets are used with English letters. Two types of Line Printers are available.

— *Drum Printers:* It consists of a cylindrical drum. The characters to be printed are embossed on its surface

— *Chain Printers:* It has a steel band on which the character sets are embossed.

Serial Printers

It prints one character at a time, with the print head moving across a line. They are similar to typewriters. They are normally slow (30 to 300 character per second). The most popular serial printer is "Dot Matrix Printer". Here a character to be printed is made up of a finite number of dots and so, the print head consists of an array of pins.

Characters to be printed are sent one character at a time from the memory to the printer. The character code is decoded by the printer electronics and activates the appropriate pins in the print head. Many dot matrix printers are bi-directional. i.e.

they print form left to right as well as from right to left on return. This enhances the speed of printing. The printing speed is around 300 characters per second.

Letter Quality Printers

Here the characters are represented by sharp continuous lines and so the output is good looking An example of such a printer is "Inkjet Printer". It consists of a print head, which has a number of small hole or nozzles. Individual holes can be heated very rapidly by an integrated circuit resistor.

When the resistor heats up, the ink near it vaporizes and is ejected through the nozzle and makes a dot on paper placed near the head. A high-resolution inkjet printer has around 50 nozzles within a height of 7mm and can print with a resolution of 300 dots per inch. Latest inkjet printers have multiple heads, on per color, which allows color printing. The printing speed is around 120 characters per second.

Laser Printers

Here an electronically controlled laser beam traces out the desired character to be printed on a photoconductive drum. The drum attracts an ink toner on o the exposed areas. This image is transferred to the paper, which comes in contact with the drum. Low speed laser printers, which can print 4 to 16 pages per minute, are now very popular and the unit cost is around Rs.0.5 lakh. Very fast printers print 10,000 lines per minute and cost per unit is around R.5 lakhs. These printers give excellent outputs and can print a variety of fonts. As these printers do not have type head striking on a ribbon, they are known as non-impact printers.

Apart from printers, the other output devices are given below:

— Drum Plotter

— Flat Bed Plotter

— Microfilm and Microfiche

— Graphic Display device (Digitizing Tablet)

— Speech Output Unit

Modem

Computers available in remote locations can communicate with each other using a telecommunication line. One way of connecting the computers is by using devices called *modems.* A modem is used to transfer data from one computer to another using the telephone lines.

A modem converts the strings of 0s and 1s into electrical signals which can be transferred over the telephone lines. Both the receiving and the transmitting computer have a telephone connection and a modem. An external modem is connected to the computer like a typical input or an output device. An internal modem is fitted into the circuitry related to the CPU and Memory.

A modem is used to translate information transferred through telephone lines or cable.

The term stands for *modulate and demodulate* which changes the signal from *digital*, which computers use, to *analog*, which telephones use and then back again. A high speed connection also requires a modem but because the information is transferred digitally it isn't required to change the signal from digital to analog but is used to create the connection between your computer and the computer you are connecting with.

Modems are measured by the speed that the information is transferred. The measuring tool is called the *baud rate.* Originally modems worked at speeds below 2400 baud but today analog speeds of 56,000 are common. Cable, wireless or digital subscriber lines (DSL) modems can transfer information much faster with rates of 300,000 baud and up.

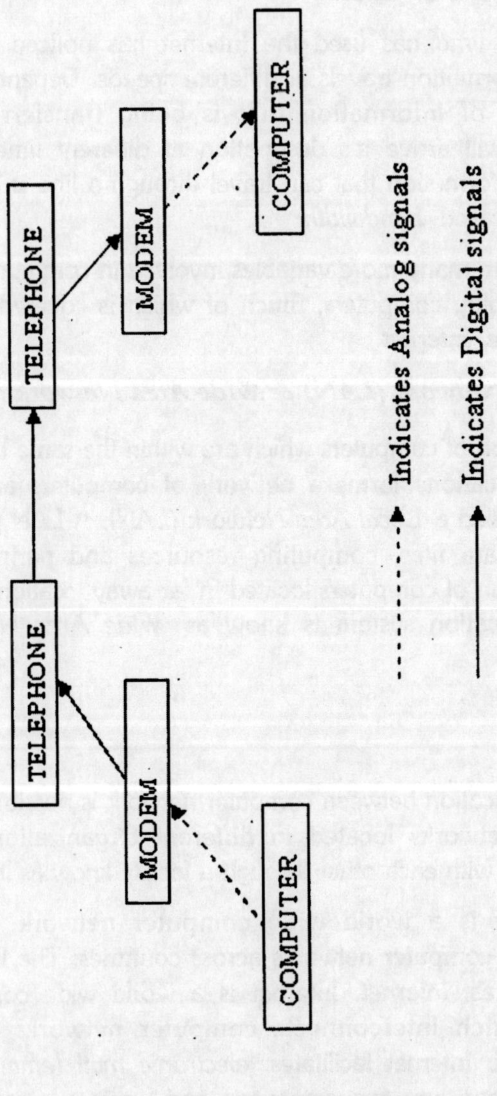

Figure 8. Computer Communication using Telephone Lines

Modems also use *Error Correction* which corrects for transmission errors by constantly checking whether the information was received properly or not and *Compression* which allows for faster data transfer rates. Information is transferred in *packets.* Each packet is checked for errors and is re-sent if there is an error.

Anyone who has used the Internet has noticed that at times the information travels at different speeds. Depending on the amount of information that is being transferred the information will arrive it's destination at different times. The amount of information that can travel through a line is limited. This limit is called *bandwidth.*

There are many more variables involved in communication technology using computers, much of which is covered in the section on the *Internet.*

Local Area Network (LAN) & Wide Area Network (WAN)

Interconnection of computers which are within the same building or nearby locations forms a network of computers and this network is called a *Local Area Network (LAN).* A LAN permits sharing of data files, computing resources and peripherals. Interconnection of computers located in far away locations using telecommunication system is know as *Wide Area Network (WAN).*

Internet

Intercommunication between computer network is possible now. Computer networks located in different Organizations can communicate with each other through a facility know as Internet.

Internet is a world wide computer network, which interconnects computer networks across countries. The Internet facility know as *Internet.* Internet is a world wide computer network, which interconnects computer networks across countries. The Internet facilitates *electronic mail (email), file-transfer* between any two computers and *remote access* to a computer connected in the internet. This intercommunication facility has changed the style of functioning of the business organization and it has made the world a global village

Scanners

Scanners allow you to transfer pictures and photographs to your computer. A scanner 'scans' the image from the top to the bottom, one line at a time and transfers it to the computer as a series of *bits* or a *bitmap*. You can then take that image and use it in a paint program, send it out as a fax or print it. With optional *Optical Character Recognition* (OCR) software you can convert printed documents such as newspaper articles to text that can be used in your word processor. Most scanners use *TWAIN* software that makes the scanner accessable by other software applications.

Digital cameras allow you to take digital photographs. The images are stored on a memory chip or disk that can be transferred to your computer. Some cameras can also capture sound and video.

Case

The case houses the microchips and circuitry that run the computer. Desktop models usually sit under the monitor and tower models beside. They come in many sizes, including desktop, mini, midi, and full tower. There is usually room inside to expand or add components at a later time. By removing the cover off the case you will may find plate covered, empty slots that allow you to add cards. There are various types of slots including IDE, ASI, USB, PCI and Firewire slots.

Notebook computers may have room to expand depending on the type of computer. Most Notebooks also have connections or ports that allows expansion or connection to exterior, peripheral devices such as monitor, portable hard-drives or other devices.

Cards

Cards are components added to computers to increase their capability. When adding a peripheral device make sure that your computer has a slot of the type needed by the device.

Sound cards allow computers to produce sound like music and voice. The older sound cards were 8 bit then 16 bit then 32 bit. Though human ear can't distinguish the fine difference between sounds produced by the more powerful sound card they allow for more complex music and music production.

Colour cards allow computers to produce colour (with a colour monitor of course). The first colour cards were 2 bit which produced 4 colours [CGA]. It was amazing what could be done with those 4 colours. Next came 4 bit allowing for 16 [EGA and VGA] colours Then came 16 bit allowing for 1064 colours and then 24 bit which allows for almost 17 million colours and now 32 bit is standard allowing monitors to display almost a billion separate colours.

Figure 9. Card

Video cards allow computers to display video and animation. Some video cards allow computers to display television as well as *capture* frames from video. A video card with a digital video camera allows computers users to produce live video. A high speed or network connection is needed for effective video transmission.

Network cards allow computers to connect together to communicate with each other. Network cards have connections for cable, thin wire or wireless networks.

Cables connect internal components to the *Motherboard*, which is a board with series of electronic path ways and connections allowing the CPU to communicate with the other components of the computer.

Memory

Memory can be very confusing but is usually one of the easiest pieces of hardware to add to your computer. It is common to confuse *chip memory* with *disk storage*. An example of the difference between memory and storage would be the difference between a table where the actual work is done (memory) and and a filing cabinet where the finished product is stored (disk). To add a bit more confusion, the computer's hard disk can be used as *temporary memory* when the program needs more than the chips can provide.

A *flip-flop* made of electronic semiconductor devices is used to fabricated a memory cell. These memory cells organized as a *Random Access Memory (RAM)*. Each cell has a capability to store one bit of information. A main memory or store of a computer is organized using a large number of cells. Each cell stores a binary digit. A memory cell, which does not loose the bit stored in it when no power is supplied to the cell, is know as a *non-volatile cell*.

A *word* is a group of bits, which are stored and retrieved as a unit. A memory system is organized to store a number of words. A *Byte* consists of 8 bits. A word may store one or more bytes. The storage capacity of a memory is the number of bytes it can store. The address of the location from where a word is to be retrieved or to be stored is entered in a *Memory Address Register (MAR)*. The data retrieved from memory or to be stored in memory are placed in a *Memory Data Register*

(MDR). The time taken to write a word is known as the Write time. The time to retrieve information is called the *Access time* of the memory.

The time taken to access a word in a memory is independent of the address of the word and hence it is know as a *Random Access Memory (RAM)*. The main memory used to store programs and data in a computer is a RAM. A RAM may be fabricated with permanently stored information, which cannot be erased. Such a memory is called a *Read Only Memory (ROM)*. For more specialized uses, a user can store his won special functions or programs in a ROM. Such ROM's are called *Programmable ROM (PROM)*. A serial access memory is organized by arranging memory cells in a linear sequence. Information is retrieved or stored in such a memory by using a read/write head. Data is presented serially for writing and is retrieved serially during read.

Random Access Memory or *RAM* is the memory that the computer uses to temporarily store the information as it is being processed. The more information being processed the more RAM the computer needs.

One of the first home computers used 64 *kilobytes* of RAM memory (Commodore 64). Today's modern computers need a minimum of 64 MB (recommended 128 MB or more) to run Windows or OS 10 with modern software.

RAM memory chips come in many different sizes and speeds and can usually be *expanded*. Older computers came with 512 KB of memory which could be expanded to a maximum of 640 KB. In most modern computers the memory can be expand by adding or replacing the memory chips depending on the processor you have and the type of memory your computer uses. Memory chips range in size from 1 MB to 512 MB. As computer technology changes the type of memory changes as well making old memory chips obsolete. Check your computer manual to find out what kind of memory your computer uses before purchasing new memory chips.

COMPUTER LANGUAGES

Machine language

The computers can execute a program written using binary digits only. This type of programs is called machine language programs. Since these programs use only '0's and '1's it will be very difficult for developing programs for complex problem solving. Also it will be very difficult for a person to understand a machine language program written by another person. At present, computer users do not write programs using machine language. Also these programs written for execution in one computer cannot be used on another type of computer. i.e., the programs were machine dependent.

Assembly Language

In assembly language *mnemonic* codes are used to develop program for problem solving. The program given below shows assembly language program to add two numbers A & B.

Program code	Description
READ A	It reads the value of A
ADD B	The value of B is added with A.
STORE C	The result is store in C.
PRINT C	The result in 'C' is printed.
HALT	Stop execution.

Assembly language is designed mainly to replace each machine code with and understandable mnemonic code. To execute an assembly language program it should first be translates into an equivalent machine language program. Writing and understanding programs in assembly language is easier than that of machine language. The programs written in assembly language are also machine dependent.

High Level Languages

High level language are developed to allow application programs, which are machine independent. High level language permits the user to use understandable codes using the language structure. In order to execute a high-level language program, it should be translated into a machine language either using a compiler or interpreter. The high level languages commonly used are *FORTRAN (FOR*mula *TRAN*slation), *BASIC* (*B*eginner's *A*ll-purpose *S*ymbolic *I*nstruction *C*ode), *COBOL* (*CO*mmon *B*usiness *O*riented *L*anguage). Recently developed programming language such as Visual Foxpro, Visual Basic (VB), Visual C++ (VC++) are more popular among the software developers. The following program written in BASIC language is to add two given numbers.

Program Code	Description
10 INPUT A,B	To read the value of A&B
20 LET C=A+B	A&B are added and result is stored in C
30 PRINT C	Print the value of C
40 END	Stop execution

SOFTWARE

The software is the information that the computer uses to get the job done. Software needs to be accessed before it can be used. There are many terms used for process of accessing software including *running*, *executing*, *starting up*, *opening*, and others.

Computer *programs* allow users to complete tasks. A program can also be referred to as an *application* and the two words are used interchangeably.

Examples of software *programs* or *applications* would be the *Operating System* (DOS, Windows 9x/Millenium/XP, O/S2, UNIX, MacOS 9.x/10.x and various others), *Wordprocessor* (typing letters), *Spreadsheet* (financial info), *Database* (inventory control and address book), *Graphics program*, *Internet Browser*, *Email* and many others.

As well any *document* that you create, graphic you design, sound you compose, file you make, letter you write, email you send or anything that you create on your computer is referred to as software. All software is stored in *files*.

Software is stored on a *disk* or *tape* whether that disk is a *floppy*, *hard disk*, *CD*, tape or one of the dozens of other *storage devices* available.

There are millions of different pieces of software available for almost every conceivable need. Software is available commercially through stores and mail order and also available on the *Internet*. Software is also available through an Open Source license which allows anyone to use the Open Source software free of charge as long as the license is maintained. If you can't find the application that you need *software development* companies can custom design software for you.

Computer software may be classified into two broad categories:

Application Software

It is the set of programs necessary to carry out operations for a specified application.

Example

Programs

— To solve a set of equations

— To process examination results

— To prepare a Pay-Bill for an organization

— To prepare Electricity-Bill for each month.

System Software

These are general program written for the system, which provide the environment to facilitate writing of Application software. Some of the system programs are given below:

— *Compiler:* It is a translator system program used to translate a High-level language program into a Machine language program.

— *Assembler:* It is another translator program used to translate an Assembly language program into a Machine language program.

— *Interpreter:* It is also a translator system program used to translate a High level language program into a Machine language program, but it translates and executes line by line.

— *Loader:* It is a system program used to store the machine language program into the memory of the computer.

The largest software companies offer packages of software or *suites* that include many of the programs that the average person or business needs. Software packages or suites contain programs that work together and share information, making it easier to combine that information in versatile ways. For example when writing a letter you can get the mailing address from an address book, include a letterhead from a graphics program and included a financial chart from a spreadsheet and combine this collection of information in the body of the letter.

The three basic types of software are; *commercial*, *shareware* and *open source* software. Some software is also release into the public domain without a license.

Commercial software comes prepackaged and is available from software stores and through the Internet.

Shareware is software developed by individual and small companies that cannot afford to market their software world wide or by a company that wants to release a demonstration version of their commercial product. You will have an evaluation period in which you can decide whether to purchase the product or not. Shareware software often is disabled in some way and has a notice attached to explain the legal requirements for using the product.

Open Source software is created by generous programmers and released into the public domain for public use. There is usually a copyright notice that must remain with the software product. Open Source software is not public domain in that the company or individual that develops the software retains ownership of the program but the software can be used freely.

Many popular Open Source applications are being developed and upgraded regularly by individuals and companies that believe in the Open Source concept.

TYPES OF COMPUTERS

There are a lot of terms used to describe computers. Most of these words imply the size, expected use or capability of the computer. While the term computer can apply to virtually any device that has a microprocessor in it, most people think of a computer as a device that receives input from the user through a mouse or keyboard, processes it in some fashion and displays the result on a screen.

Personal computer (PC)

The personal computer (PC) defines a computer designed for general use by a single person. While a Mac is a PC, most people relate the term with systems that run the Windows operating system. PCs were first known as microcomputers because they were a complete computer but built on a smaller scale than the huge systems in use by most businesses.

Figure 10. Hand-held (HPC)

Figure 11. Tablet PC

Desktop

A PC that is not designed for portability. The expectation with desktop systems are that you will set the computer up in a permanent location. Most desktops offer more power, storage and versatility for less cost than their portable brethren.

Figure 12. Desktop

Laptop

Also called notebooks, laptops are portable computers that integrate the display, keyboard, a pointing device or trackball, processor, memory and hard drive all in a battery-operated package slightly larger than an average hardcover book.

Figure 13. Laptop

Palmtop

More commonly known as Personal Digital Assistants (PDAs), palmtops are tightly integrated computers that often use flash memory instead of a hard drive for storage. These computers usually do not have keyboards but rely on touchscreen technology for user input. Palmtops are typically smaller than a paperback novel, very lightweight with a reasonable battery life. A slightly larger and heavier version of the palmtop is the handheld computer.

Figure 14. Personal Digital Assistants (PDAs)

Workstation

A desktop computer that has a more powerful processor, additional memory and enhanced capabilities for performing a special group of task, such as 3D Graphics or game development.

Figure 15. Workstation

Server

The term server actually refers to a computer's function rather than to a specific kind of computer. A server runs a network of computers. It handles the sharing of equipment like printers and the communication between computers on the network. For such tasks a computer would need to be somewhat more capable than a desktop computer. It would need:

— more power

— larger memory

— larger storage capacity

— high speed communications

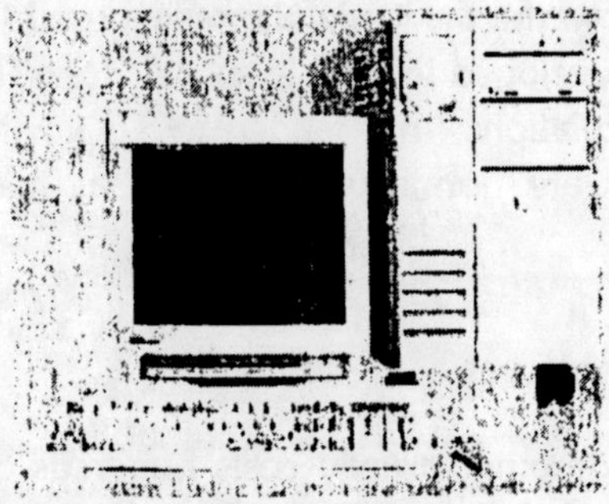

Figure 16. Server

Mainframe

In the early days of computing, mainframes were huge computers that could fill an entire room or even a whole floor! As the size of computers has diminished while the power has increased, the term mainframe has fallen out of use in favor of enterprise server. You'll still hear the term used, particularly in large companies to describe the huge machines processing millions of transactions every day.

Figure 17. Mainframe

Minicomputer

The minicomputer has become less important since the PC has gotten so powerful on its own. In fact, the ordinary new PC is much more powerful than minicomputers used to be. Originally this size was developed to handle specific tasks, like engineering and CAD calculations, that tended to tie up the main frame. Minicomputers are normally referred to as mid-range servers now.

Supercomputer

This type of computer usually costs hundreds of thousands or even millions of dollars. Although some supercomputers are single computer systems, most are comprised of multiple high performance computers working in parallel as a single system. The best known supercomputers are built by Cray Supercomputers.

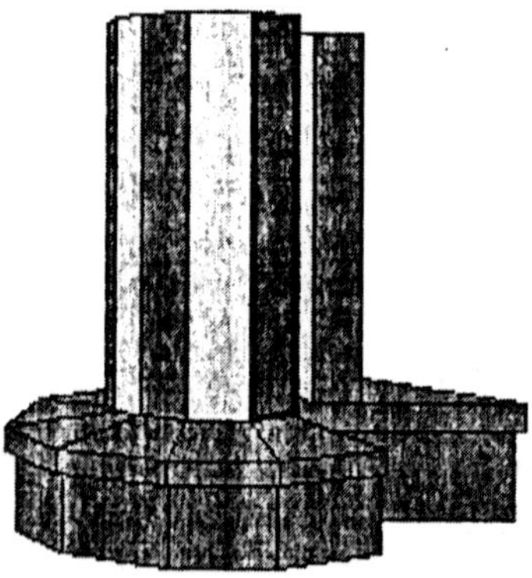

Figure 18. Supercomputers

Tower

The tower and the smaller mini-tower style cases have become popular as people started needing more room for extra drives inside. Repairmen certainly appreciate the roominess inside for all the cables and circuit boards and their knuckles.

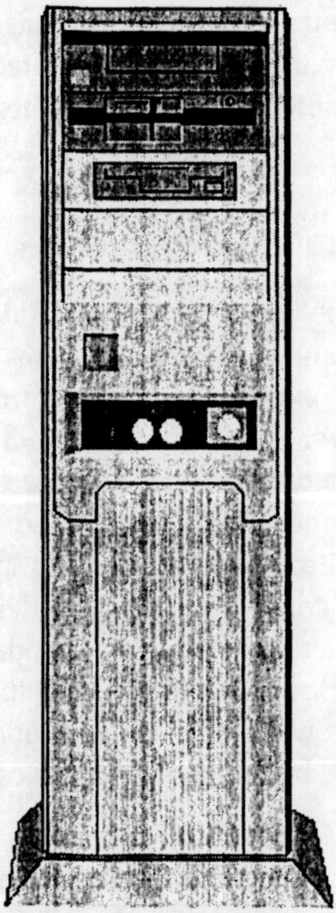

Figure 19. Tower

Wearable

The latest trend in computing is wearable computers. Essentially, common computer applications (e-mail, database, multimedia, calendar/scheduler) are integrated into watches, cell phones, visors and even clothing.

Distributed or Grid Computing

The power needed for some calculations is more than even a single supercomputer can manage. In distributed computing using a PC grid many computers of all sizes can work on parts of the problem and their results are pooled. A number of current projects rely on volunteers with computers connected to the Internet. The computers do the work when they are not busy otherwise.

COMPUTER AIDED LEARNING (CAL)

CAL is an abbreviation of Computer Aided Learning and is one of the most commonly used acronyms within education. It is difficult to say exactly when the term "CAL" was first employed, however since the mid 1980s CAL has been increasingly used to describe the use of technology in teaching. But what exactly does "Computer Aided Learning" refer to? Well there is, despite the ever increasing interest in the use of technology within education, no clear definition of the term "CAL". It does not refer to a given standardised set of rules, HCI ideals or generic specification. So in the absence of a type description perhaps we should concern ourselves less with the meaning of "CAL" but rather with the context in which the term is used.

There are two common contexts of usage: CAL as Computer Based Learning and CAL as Integrative Technology.

Difference between CAL and CBL

In the absence of a classical definition "CAL" has often been used to describe the development and application of educational technology for a variety of circumstances. From the mid 1980s until the early 1990s the term CAL was often used to refer to the development of either a single computer program or a series of programs which replaced the more traditional methods of instruction, in particular the lecture. This was in fact a natural progression from an early misguided strategy, propounded by Government literature), which encouraged through ignorance the development of computer programs with the explicit aim of replacing current methods as opposed to their incorporation within the traditional setting together with support to or from existing methods.

More attention was being paid to solving the current staff to student ratio crisis rather than improving the quality of student education through the re-evaluation of the current methods of instruction. This would have resulted in a coherent instructional strategy within which CAL would form a part. Under these circumstances, whereby a computer program replaces a specific part or the whole of a lecture course with no provision or support provided from other methods, we are actually encouraging Computer Based Learning (CBL).

CBL involves the development of a computer program with no provision, intentional or otherwise, for the re-evaluation of the current methods of teaching and the subject itself. CAL produced under these conditions is actually a computer program whose content consists of little more than lecture notes. Thus Computer Based Learning is exactly that.

We are using the medium of the computer as the primary means of knowledge exposition with no support or reference to other methods of instruction – the computer is the sole basis for learning. Under these circumstances where a lecture has either been replaced or added to by a program (i.e. a "bolt on" computer application) which has been developed under a strategy lacking in re-evaluation then only the medium of instruction has changed. The lecturer has simply re-produced their lecture notes and displayed them in another format.

However CBL does have its place within the curriculum, mainly as CBL in the classic sense where lecture notes are displayed in electronic format, e.g. a web page. There are several advantages in comparison to the more traditional methods, in particular the standard lecture and text book. For example a web page may be accessed at any time and over any distance; there are no limits over access unlike a library book; the entire content of the course - the lecturer's perception of the topic is completely available and the content can be easily modified and updated.

However such advantages are in the main concerned with resources rather than actual learning. Only the fact that the entire content of the course is presented has a bearing on the quality of learning, however the communication between tutor and student is one sided with little opportunity for the student to express their views of the topic.

So learning technology when used in this context is CBL rather than CAL. However is it possible to change CBL into CAL? The answer is yes. A small step in the right direction is to add some form of formative or even summative assessment areas where the student can check their conception of the topic and hence their progress through the material. For example simple multiple choice questions (MCQ).

However this only a start. What is actually required is subject based re-evaluation which will determine the learning outcomes expected of the technology and their methods of assessment. This will remove the material from that of a CBL context and place it within a CAL one.

CAL as integrative technology

"CAL" has also been used to describe a relatively more integrative approach whereby the program does not actually replace a lecture but is introduced into the course as a learning resource. Here the students experience directed learning (directed by the lecturer) or self study which takes place "outside" the main curriculum hours, (i.e. the primary contact hours between student and tutor), and thus beyond any level of support from traditional methods. In fact the term CAL used in this context describes little more than an "add on" or "bolt on" resource for student self study whose success in terms of usage is dependent upon a number of student centred factors, not least their self discipline and motivation. So although there appears to be an attempt to integrate the program to form a part of a multi instructional media learning environment the truth of the matter is that it has been bolted on and is more akin to CBL.

The contexts outlined above refer to two common types of "CAL" mis-usage whereby the term is used erroneously to describe educational methods which are little more than CBL. Both contexts involve a computer program which is essentially "on its own" - not supported within a framework of instructional methods which would have only come about through a general re-evaluation of the educational strategy employed to teach a particular subject.

Truth of CAL

In the absence of a clear definition what *should* the term "CAL" actually refer to? The use of a single program within the class room? In the past developers have used the term "CAL" when describing the creation and performance of a computer program particularly those used as a library-type resource. This is in fact a common misinterpretation of "CAL" and example of its misuse.

Computer Aided Learning describes an educational environment where a computer program, or an application as they are commonly known, is used to *assist* the user in learning a particular subject. The key issue is the word assist which means that the program is not alone in this aim and that there are other methods involved.

CAL according to our usage of the term refers to an overall integrative approach of instructional methods and is actually part of the bigger picture. When used in this context CAL describes an integrated approach to teaching a subject in which learning technology forms a part and which only comes about after re-assessment of the current teaching methods. This is Computer Aided Learning - in that the computer, being a program of some sort, is an *aid* to an overall learning strategy – which in itself is a conglomeration of other methods of instruction, (e.g. the lecture, tutorial sheets, text books etc.). So CAL is not a single computer program but art of an educational strategy devised to teach a particular subject.

The relative part each method of instruction plays within the strategy is determined through the re-evaluation of the subject being taught. Re evaluation examines the educational objectives of the subject and their associated learning outcomes and determines the success with which the current methods of teaching and assessment are achieving them in terms of knowledge gain. Thus re-evaluation helps to determine the areas or objectives of the subject in which the traditional methods are failing and where the computer program can help. Furthermore re evaluation determines the level at which the program operates – the educational objectives which the program alone cannot teach and thus the level of required support from the other methods. Thus re evaluation results in a coherent educational strategy within which each instructional method compliments and supports the other ensuring that no area of the subject is overlooked.

2

COMPUTERS IN EDUCATION: INSTRUCTION DESIGN AND TECHNOLOGY

WAYS OF USING COMPUTERS IN EDUCATION

Recent innovations in the use of the computer in education are as an information gatherer, a communications device, and a publishing medium.

The computer as an information gatherer

Vast amounts of information are now held in machine-readable form on both CD-ROMs and the Internet and this brings with it many advantages and some disadvantages. The main advantages are that:

— Students have access to an almost limitless amount of information compared with the traditional resource of text books and a few books on a specific topic in the library.

— While it can take a considerable time to publish a book or even a journal, information on the Web can be published very quickly and, in some cases, as an event occurs. Information from the Net can, therefore, be much more up to date than that obtained from printed materials.

— Using these media, students can gain valuable information processing skills.

Among the disadvantages are:

— Because of the vast amount of information available, students can go into 'information overload' unless they develop the appropriate skills to deal with it.

— Many of the traditional mechanisms in place to ensure the validity of published materials do not exist as far as the Internet is concerned and students must be shown how to validate information before using it. This situation is compounded by the fact that we have learnt to believe that information from a computer is always true and so students must be taught the saying "Garbage in, garbage out" as anyone can publish anything on the Net.

— Even graphical images published on the Net may not be accurate as with modern, high end graphics programs, it is possible to manipulate images in many ways and for changes to be undetectable.

— As it is so easy to cut and paste information from an electronic source, it will be necessary to review the type of assessment that is undertaken to ensure that students present their own work which is a product of their own thinking and effort.

As a publisher of student work

Traditionally, when a student has produced a good piece of work, it has been 'published' by displaying it on the classroom wall. However, with the advent of the Web, schools can now publish students' work so that it can, potentially, be read by anyone in the world. If students know that their work is going to be viewed by such a large audience, they must be motivated to produce their best work.

An example of students' work published on the Web is that of a class at Murrurindi Public School. This site represents a considerable amount of hard work and learning by these students as they had to undertake the research, learn how to produce and design HTML pages, take and manipulate digital photographs, and produce pages and images that could be downloaded quickly (their first set of pages contained images that were far too large and so took a long time to download).

An additional advantage of students publishing their work on the Net is that an increasingly large body of child-centred material will become available. A major problem with the use of the Net by schools is that the vast majority of information available is written by adults for adults. Publishing work by students and teachers could help alleviate this.

The computer as a communications device

One of the most powerful aspects of using the computer in the classroom is as a communications device. For years teachers have tried to set up systems where students could communicate with those in other countries, but with limited success. The cost of overseas telephone calls mitigated against this being an option, while post has proved to be so slow that students very quickly lost their motivation for the projects due to the excessive time involved in waiting for a reply.

The Internet offers almost instantaneous, low cost communication with people in most countries of the world. It also offers a variety of media that can be used, including:

— e-mail: this allows students to correspond with other young people throughout the world, and in some cases experts in specific areas, and even occasionally Transantarctic explorers. While e-mail is textual, other media such as graphics, audio and video can also be sent as attachments.

— Chat: allows real time communication. While many chat lines are adult orientated and probably not suitable for children, there are specific kids chat lines available.

— Newsgroups: bulletin board systems. While many of these are unsuitable for use by children, those made available by NSW DET's ISP (Oz-email) are 'kid-safe'.

The main disadvantages of these systems are that

(a) students can access unsuitable systems and

(b) children can be contacted by unsavoury individuals whose identity is protected by the anonymous nature of the Internet.

Research on the effectiveness of educational software

Research into the effectiveness of computer based instruction in the learning process is inconclusive. Some reports indicate that CBI brings about a great improvement in the learning process while others equate its effectiveness with more traditional forms of learning. It seems strange that so much money and resources are being ploughed into the use of computers in the educational system while there is so little evidence to show that they are effective. A number of reasons can be put forward to suggest why there is a lack of evidence to support their use:

— Computers have been in use in the education system for a comparatively short time and during this period there have been major and continuing changes in the available technology. As, by its very nature, research and evaluation must lag behind the introduction of new technology, most research is out of date before it is released.

— Little funding is made available for educational research

— Many people involved in the development of educational software do not take time out to evaluate what has already been done as there is a constant battle to keep up with new initiatives.

— Many researchers who are not technologically competent do not feel equipped to evaluate the use of computers in education and so do not undertake studies in this area, but any contribution that they made would probably be more valuable than that of people trying to advance the use of technology in education.

INSTRUCTIONAL DESIGN

Instructional design as a process

Instructional Design is the systematic development of instructional specifications using learning and instructional theory to ensure the quality of instruction. It is the entire process of analysis of learning needs and goals and the development of a delivery system to meet those needs. It includes development of instructional materials and activities; and tryout and evaluation of all instruction and learner activities.

Instructional design as a discipline:

Instructional Design is that branch of knowledge concerned with research and theory about instructional strategies and the process for developing and implementing those strategies.

Instructional design as a science

Instructional design is the science of creating detailed specifications for the development, implementation, evaluation, and maintenance of situations that facilitate the learning of both large and small units of subject matter at all levels of complexity.

Instructional design as reality

Instructional design can start at any point in the design process. Often a glimmer of an idea is developed to give the core of an instruction situation. By the time the entire process is done the designer looks back and she or he checks to see that all parts of the "science" have been taken into account. Then the entire process is written up as if it occurred in a systematic fashion.

Instructional system

An instructional system is an arrangement of resources and procedures to promote learning. Instructional design is the systematic process of developing instructional systems and instructional development is the process of implementing the system or plan.

Instructional technology

Instructional technology is the systemic and systematic application of strategies and techniques derived from behavioral, cognitive, and constructivist theories to the solution of instructional problems.

Instructional technology is the systematic application of theory and other organized knowledge to the task of instructional design and development.

Instructional Technology = Instructional Design + Instructional Development

Instructional Ddevelopment

The process of implementing the design plans.

COMPUTER-ASSISTED INSTRUCTION (CAI)

Computer-assisted instruction was first used in education and training during the 1950s. Early work was done by IBM and such people as Gordon Pask, and O.M. Moore, but CAI grew rapidly in the 1960s when federal funding for research and development in education and industrial laboratories was implemented. The U.S. government wanted to determine the possible effectiveness of computer-assisted instruction, so they developed two competing companies, (Control Data Corporation and Mitre Corporation) who came up with the PLATO and TICCIT projects. Despite money and research, by the mid seventies it was apparent that CAI was not going to be the success that people had believed. Some of the reasons are:

CAI had been oversold and could not deliver. lack of support from certain sectors. technical problems in implementation. lack of quality software. high cost.

Computer-assisted instruction was very much drill-and-practice - controlled by the program developer rather than the learner. Little branching of instruction was implemented although TICCIT did allow the learner to determine the sequence of instruction or to skip certain topics.

COMPUTER-BASED TOOLS FOR INSTRUCTIONAL DESIGN

Computer-based tools for instructional design (ID) help designers or teachers to perform one or more of the various activities that can be organized according to the ADDIE model, that is the analysis, design, development or production, implementation and evaluation of instructional systems.

The history of computer-based ID tools is closely linked to the history of computer-based instruction. After it has been decided to use the computer as the primary instructional medium, or to develop computer-based instruction, it is an evident step to use the computer not only for the delivery but also for the production of the instruction.

Consequently, research and development work in the field of ID tools has been dominated, and still is dominated, by *authoring tools* for the development or production of computer-based instruction. Many of those systems are commercially available (e.g., ToolBook, Macromedia Director, Authorware, etc.) and dedicated systems for authoring Web-based instruction, which is currently the most popular form of computer-based instruction, are rapidly appearing on the market.

But until now, there has been less interest in computer-based ID tools that support the analysis and design activities that are undertaken *before* a final medium selection is made and the instruction, which may be *not* computerbased, is actually produced. In addition, there has also been little interest in computer-based ID tools that support the implementation and evaluation activities that are undertaken *after* the instruction has been developed.

Importance of Computer-based ID tools

The term *new learning* is used to refer to a broad array of instructional approaches that are all characterized by their focus on rich, multidisciplinary and often collaborative learning tasks (called cases, projects, problems, etc.) that are somehow representative for authentic, real-life tasks. The tasks should ensure active learning and integrate multiple learning objectives in a meaningful way.

In addition, collaborative learning tasks offer the opportunity for negotiation between students and take advantage of the fact that multiple perspectives on reality exist, which may enrich the learning experience. From a task-analytical point of view, new learning thus asks for more powerful techniques that can deal with real-life tasks and, especially, complex sets of integrated learning objectives. And from a design point of view it should be clear that the design of practice and in particular the design of meaningful whole tasks, is given precedence over the—traditional—design of to-bepresented information. Both changes contribute to an increased complexity of the design process and the resulting instructional systems.

Other changes may be less central but are still of utmost importance to the nature of the design process.

First, the multidisciplinary character of learning tasks indicates that ID is no longer aimed at stand-alone "one-teacher" courses, but often needs to rely on the expertise of more teachers and must fit into the (re)design of a whole curriculum within an educational organization. A comprehensive contextual analysis is needed to clarify the context and identify all stakeholders involved.

Second, traditional target group analysis must be refined in order to cope with personalized and individualized forms of instruction, which are needed to develop truly learner-centered instructional systems.

Third, the focus on self-directed learning and the desire to make students responsible for their own learning processes requires a thorough analysis of higher-order skills such as self-regulation and self-assessment, and also confronts the designer with the difficult task to intertwine the ID for these higher-order skills with the basic design for domain-related firstorder skills.

And to conclude, the increased use of information and communication technology (ICT) in instructional systems has its own new problems and design challenges (e.g., Tabbers, Martens, & van Merriënboer, in press). It requires a balanced approach to finding an optimal medium mix, instead of simply selecting one primary medium.

Thus, new learning has important effects on the design of instructional systems and in general increases the complexity of design processes. Several measures may be taken to effectively deal with this. For instance, most researchers agree that the simple, linear version of the ADDIE model is not useful to conduct complex design enterprises. Rapid prototyping approaches or highly flexible, "zigzag" design approaches seem to be more apt for the design of new learning environments.

Furthermore, ID is becoming more and more a collaborative task. On the one hand, design teams are needed that consist of instructional designers, content experts, and teachers, who provide multidisciplinary input,and often graphical artists, and programmers. On the other hand, a much larger group of stakeholders (e.g., educational managers, field experts, branch representatives, etc.) needs to be involved in order to take care of organizational constraints and consequences.

All these changes to the design process require at least a good information management, making sure that intermediate and final design products are clearly linked to each other, stored in well-organized databases, easily accessible and changeable for all parties involved, and so forth. It is our firm conviction that computerbased ID tools may help to do so.

Sample of Computer-based ID tools

An increasing number of researchers believe that computer-based ID tools can play an important role in resolving some of the problems and difficulties that occur in ID. Recent review articles of computer- based ID tools describe a broad range of ID tools, including so-called "preauthoring systems" that support needs assessment (e.g., Advisor P.I.) or the whole analysis and design process (e.g., Advanced Instructional Design Advisor or AIDA, Designer's Edge, Langevin Instructional DesignWare), systems for the selection of methods and media (e.g., Training Delivery Assessment Model, Automated Media Selection Model), and systems for supporting the implementation and evaluation of instructional systems (e.g., CASCADE-EVAL).

The ID tools do not differ only with regard to the specific analysis and design activities that they support, but also on a large number of other dimensions. Nieveen and Gustafson provided a useful conceptual framework to compare ID tools, with the five dimensions:

(a) development process and theory,

(b) intended output,

(c) purpose and evidence,

(d) intended users, and

(e) task support.

The dimension development process and theory pertains to the phase or phases in the design process that are supported by the tool (A, D, D, I, E or combinations). The underlying theory, if any, can be a broad paradigm.

The dimension *intended output* pertains to the desired results of the activities that are supported, for instance, a concept tree of lesson contents, a training blueprint, a lesson plan, an evaluation plan, or a particular medium choice. The dimension *purpose and evidence* pertains to the main purpose of the tool, such as speeding up the design process, increasing the cost effectiveness, or improving the quality of to-be-designed products.

Evidence reflects the data that are available to support the claimed benefits in terms of validity, practicality and effectiveness. The dimension *intended users* refers to the function or role of the users (e.g., professional designers, teachers, learners, school management, etc.) as well as specific characteristics that are necessary to effectively work with the ID tool, such as computer experience, design experience, and so forth.

Of particular interest for our current purpose is the fifth dimension, namely *task support.* ID tools can be seen as a special type of electronic performance support system, that is, interactive computer-based tools that provide on-the-job, just-in-time support to facilitate task performance or product development. They can be designed to give four basic types of support:

(a) library and information support, by providing useful resources and databases,

(b) *standardization* support, by providing rules, regulations and directions for performing specific tasks,

(c) full or partial *task automation*, by providing automated tools, expert systems and wizards, and

(d) *instruction*, by providing users just-in-time learning materials that may help to perform their tasks.

Many means of support may be distinguished for each of the basic types, including checklists, cue cards, glossaries and dictionaries, diagrams, examples, intelligent agents and wizards, frequently asked questions, how-to procedures, references, templates, tutorials, and much more.

Computer-animations as Learning Objects

During the last decades the availability of educational software has grown steadily. An obvious tendency is the increased incorporation of sophisticated animations within educational multimedia. Their enhanced implementation seems to be justified since the educational advantage of animations has been proven in different studies. However, the creation of computer-animations is time consuming and expensive. Given the educational potential together with the time consuming creation highlights the necessity and importance of using computer animations as learning objects in order to ensure efficient reusability.

Since many computer-animations are self-contained, even if they are embedded within complex hypermedia learning environments, the possibility to use them as learning objects is high. In order to ensure a high educational power the instructional design has to be adopted appropriately. Lowe, however, states that intuition and artistic judgment appear to be the dominant guiding forces for designing animations. This statement is especially underlined by the tendency to embed costly 3D-animations in educational software although the educational advantage of 3D-animations over 2D-animations has not been proven explicitly until now.

The creation of computer animations is relatively costly and time consuming. However, their educational power is high if designed properly. It is therefore of increasing importance to establish animations with optimal instructional design properties. Commercial e-learning tools show an enhanced tendency to incorporate 3D-animations although their production is rather costly as compared to the productions of 2D-animations. Until now, producing state of the art 3Danimations requires complex and expensive software tools and specialized trained people. The creation of 2D-animations is relatively easy and can be achieved by the use of less expensive and therefore more widespread software tools.

2D-animations can be as good as 3D-animations or even better in supporting learning. Therefore, it is not necessary to restrict the adoption of learning objects to sophisticated 3D-animations. Students with high prior domain knowledge learned better with a two-dimensional animation whereas students with low prior knowledge performed similar with the 2D and the 3D-animation.

The study of Kalyuga et al. emphasizes that experienced users need less instructional cues. Additional information led to reduced learning results because these information sources were not necessary and resulted therefore in a higher cognitive load that interferes with the learning process.

Whereas costs and benefits of a three-dimensional graphical solution balance each other for low knowledge students, three-dimensional information is not necessary in experienced students. A plain two-dimensional animation is therefore sufficient for understanding and reduces redundant information that otherwise leads to additional cognitive load and hence a reduced learning success. The adoption of carefully created 2Danimations for reuse as learning object seems to be justified since their instructional design properties have a high educational value.

WEB-BASED INSTRUCTION DESIGN

Khan defines Web-Based Instruction (WBI) as: "...a hypermedia-based instructional program which utilizes the attributes and resources of the World Wide Web to create a meaningful learning environment where learning is fostered and supported."

Relan and Gillami define WBI as: "...the application of a repertoire of cognitively oriented instructional strategies within a constructivist and collaborative learning environment, utilizing the attributes and resources of the World Wide Web."

Web-Based Instruction, also called Web-Based Training, is defined by Clark as: "Individualized instruction delivered over public or private computer networks and displayed by a Web browser. WBT is not downloaded CBT, but rather on-demand training stored in a server and accessed across a network. Web-based training can be updated very rapidly, and access to training controlled by the training provider."

Though the above definitions are not identical, there is a common theme, which is that WBI takes advantage of the Internet and World Wide Web to deliver information.

Importance of WBI

WBI, which is an emerging field in education, is nevertheless, a part of the rapid growth that is the Internet. Reasons for the growth of WBI include: promotes growth of distance education economically (reliable and inexpensive source)as compared to computer based training, live broadcasts, video tapes, and so on, enables learners who prefer or are required to learn outside traditional classrooms to attend classes at their homes or offices and provides delivery medium, content provider, and subject matter in one package, unlike other mediums, such as computer based training, that require a separate delivery mechanism.

Nichols predicts that: "The potential benefit from formulating evaluation methodologies for the Web [for instructional materials] depends on whether or not the Web will become a permanent medium or a passing fad? In fact, the Web will likely soon become the most popular medium for the delivery of distance education type materials."

Design issues

The literature supports the assertion that WBI is a growing trend. The literature also indicates that a critical factor to the success of WBI is the incorporation of usability design into the development process.

The design issues gleaned from the literature review include: transfer of existing course material, as is, to WBI, without considering using the medium's capabilities, such as graphics or communications, like listservers; ignore the forms and styles required by the medium, such as using the structure of a traditional lecture course as the structure for a WBI course and use existing course material and while ignoring features without restructuring existing material to fit the features, which can lead to the student learning less.

The above examples describe how the content of instructional materials can be underutilized by simply "porting" the materials from one medium to another without considering whether the medium requires a different design approach. And along these lines, usability design is also a critical factor for successful WBI design.

Usability issues in the design of WBI include: lack of interest in interface design since authoring systems are expected to provide attractive and easy to user interfaces; need to replicate the best of the classroom environment and distance education but improve on those environments by taking advantage of Web capabilities, focus on learners and their tasks, not just the content to be taught; use of Web characteristics that are unlike traditional software applications, such as access to interfaces which cannot be controlled by the application, and the incorporation of screen and interface design at the same time the course is being designed and developed.

Boling and Sousa state that: "If people cannot use what is being delivered to them, or if they will not use it because it fails to support them in crucial ways, the promise of technology is subverted before it can begin to be fulfilled...training groups with direct responsibility for learning outcomes can not afford to lose a measure of learner motivation to poor interface decisions, or to a lack of awareness that these design issues must be addressed."

Methodology Design

Although the literature review revealed many issues in WBI design, such as can existing materials be "ported" to a WBI course without change, the literature review also revealed that many educators take user interface design for granted or are ill-prepared to create computer based training since educators often work alone or lack formal training. Additionally, poor interface design can prevent students from learning.

Another, less obvious reason for this emphasis on user interface design, is that a WBI course, can be considered a software application and also a Web Site. As McManus states: "The Web [and WBI] is delivery medium, content provider, and subject matter all in one." And like any well-designed software application or Web Site, good user interface design is crucial.

Top Ten Web Design Mistakes

Nielsen's Top Ten Web Design Mistakes are adapted from Nielsen's Alertbox. These design guides will be used to evaluate the user interface of the WBI. Note: The following is an succinct explanation of each item.

— *Using Frames.* Frames are not to be used as frames make it hard to correctly set a bookmark.

— *Gratuitous Use of Bleeding-Edge Technology.* Like avoiding to many fonts, new technology, such as three- dimensional designs should only be used if the content dictates use, such as a web site for maps. Scrolling Text, Marquees, and Constantly Running Animations. Do not include any element that constantly is moving because this distracts the reader.

— *Complex User Resource Locations (URLs).* Users may want to type in a URL directly within their browser or may use the URL as bookmark. Therefore URL should make sense and use lower case characters to make entering the data easier. Orphan Pages. Each page should have a link to the home page (index page). A page that does not allow you to navigate from the page is considered orphaned. Or a page that causes the Web Browser to display a message stating the link is no longer valid.

— *Long Scrolling Pages.* Nielsen states that "Only 10 percent of users scroll beyond the information that is visible on the screen when a page comes up." Therefore, if a page must be longer than one page, then the most important information must be displayed at the top of the page.

— *Lack of Navigation Support.* A map must be provided of how to access information on a web site and also each page should include a link to get to the next page or the previous page. Additionally, a search engine should be provided to enable users to search any page on a web site.

— *Non-Standard Link Colors.* Nilesen states that: "Links to pages that have not been seen by the user are blue; links to previously seen pages are purple or red.". This is typical throughout the World Wide Web community.

— *Outdated Information.* Information must be kept updated as information on the World Wide Web is often outdated, within days. Information considered 'old' by users may lead the user's to believe all of the information is outdated. Overly Long Download Times. Nielsen states that: "Traditional human factors guidelines indicate 10 seconds as the maximum response time before users lose interest. On the web, users have been trained to endure so much suffering that it may be acceptable to increase this limit to 15 seconds for a few pages."

APPLICATIONS OF TECHNOLOGY-BASED INSTRUCTION

Technology can help students develop positive cooperative learning relationships, enabling them to work together while researching topics and creating presentations. In such relationships, students help each other learn. Students with special needs may require more coaching in computer-based activities, but they will benefit from the experience of learning with and from other students. Traditionally, however, schools have not focused on technology as a means to support engaged learning. When computers are present in schools sersving at-risk students, they usually are used for drill-and-practice programs on basic skills rather than as tools to support students in designing their own projects.

Schools typically promote learning with technology through the use of stand-alone devices or environments. The knowledge or practice opportunity is put in the computer box or on the videotape. Students work with didactic technology applications, which are designed to teach specific skills. They interact with the technology individually (in the case of computers) or as a whole class (in the case of videotapes and other audiovisual presentations). The technology developers have control of the content. Today, educational researchers are calling for very different uses of technology. They promote classroom learning activities in which students work in small groups rather than in isolation or as a whole class.

The technologies used in the classroom are not those designed explicitly to teach basic skills, but rather are real-world applications that support research, design, analysis, composition, and communication. Technology has tremendous power to help students obtain, organize, manipulate, and display information. Students can use technology tools (such as word processing, database, design, and graphing software) in the same ways as do professionals in business, communications, and research. Such practical uses of technology contrast sharply with the more didactic technology applications designed explicitly for instruction.

Using technology for meaningful activities also helps integrate a variety of disciplines, more closely resembling activities that people undertake in the world beyond the classroom. For example, word processing is a real-world technology that can help students develop writing and thinking skills.

Using the computer, students write longer, more complex sentences and are more willing to revise and edit their work; they are able to concentrate on the thoughts they want to express rather than the mechanical skills of penmanship, spelling, and grammar. Many changes will be necessary if schools are to provide such exciting, technology-supported activities for all students. Time, effort, and resources are needed to bring students to a level of computer literacy.

At-risk children from low-income families are less likely to have access to computers in their homes and often attend schools with less computer equipment. Furthermore, schools serving large numbers of at-risk children often lack the funds and resources to support technology. School facilities must be upgraded to support technology networking.

After technologies are obtained, school districts need to ensure that all students have technological equity and equal access to the learning tools of the 21st century. Obtaining the technology for schools serving at-risk students is just the tip of the iceberg. Larger issues concern staff development needs. Because students often receive computer-based instruction in a separate computer lab, regular classroom teachers may have little contact with the technology.

Teachers need support not just for learning to use new technologies but also for acquiring skills in designing and implementing high-quality, student-centered projects. Teachers also need a strong system of professional development and ongoing support if they are to achieve the dramatic changes in teaching approaches called for by the reform movement. Rules of thumb for professional development are useful for ensuring that teachers have adequate opportunities for professional development in technology.

3

Working with Computers to Enhance Interactive Teaching and Learning Skills

INTERACTION FOR COMPUTER-AIDED LEARNING

Today, computing power is no longer a limitation for implementation of learning tools. The problem has moved from how to implement to what tools to implement and why. Current research on computer aided learning (CAL) is very focused on how to represent the learning content and tends to neglect the impact of the user-interface in the learning process. Interface design can be theory driven (the particular theory may be task related) or based on human centred design principles. In the first case, theory guides implementation as, for example, in Gibson's perceptual approach; the constructivistic approach; the activity theory; or the information processing approach, a theory of implicit and explicit learning.

The second case, i.e. the human centred design approach, strives for an interface that is attractive, easy and effective for the users. The desktop metaphor is a typical product of this approach. Other tasks that take advantage of this approach are file manipulation, text editing, or use of public automats (e.g. information kiosks, ticket vending machines, etc.). Although this approach also makes use of knowledge from different cognitive theories, research in this field is often characterised by comparative heuristic studies where particular interface features are tested for efficiency and satisfaction. Complex computer mediated problem solving can take great advantage of interfaces that are designed from considerations that run deeper than simple user friendliness.

The human centred design approach is not enough when an interface must support a task that goes beyond desktop handling. In complex tasks (e.g. computer-aided learning, computer-aided design, programming or process control) the user-interface becomes a part of the task solving process. HCI is a complex domain in which information can be channelled through the human information processing system in subtle ways.

A comparison of the user centred approach with the theoretical approach showed that a consequent application of one of the approaches would result in different suggestions for interaction design. In general, the theoretical approach resulted in interfaces that improved learning performance, but these interfaces were not necessarily most time effective. On the other hand, the application of user-centred design principles resulted in interfaces that benefited from shorter task solving times and higher satisfaction, but this was at the cost of the learning performance. A combination of both design principles would aim at defining interfaces supporting both high performance and high satisfaction.

IMPLICIT AND EXPLICIT LEARNING

The application of theory in the interface design process enables us to understand interaction in a wider context and to include task related factors in the interaction concept. The implicit and explicit learning theory was applied to different ways of communicating information in HCI; i.e. through various interaction tools, navigation methods and feedback forms. Different HCI factors become a part of the information process in CAL. The theory of implicit and explicit learning helps us to understand how this complex information process takes place. There is increasing evidence that people can learn in two different modes. An explicit learning mode is characterised by rational, selective and conscious attention.

Explicit learning implies observing a manageable number of variables from the environment and keeping count only of the contingencies between those variables. This learning mode is more demanding for the cognitive system. People who learn explicitly seem to do so by developing a mental model of the problem, which can be consulted, manipulated and communicated. Implicit learning is an unconscious process that yields abstract knowledge. Implicit learning is similar to trial and error learning. It implies storing all the contingencies between all the variables at play. Reber defines implicit learning as "a general, modal-free process, a fundamental operation whereby critical co-variations in the stimulus environment are picked up".

The success of employing one of these modes depends on characteristics of the problem or the learning task. Every learning task or problem has a structure or rules, which essentially influence how the task should be solved and which solutions should be attempted. The task saliency refers to how obvious the rules or the structure are. The saliency (or complexity) of a problem is, in this research tradition, defined as the essential problem feature accounting for success when learning in one of the two modes. Saliency is defined by the degree to which the critical features of the stimulus material are obvious to the subjects, and by the amount of information that needs to be considered. These two factors are related: the more features that need to be considered, the less salient is the problem because it is more difficult to keep track of the critical features.

The saliency of a problem increases if the number of irrelevant factors in the situation is low, or if the key events are in accordance with general knowledge from outside the problem. One example is given by Reber. They developed an artificial language consisting of strings of letters. Only certain combinations of the letters would follow the rules of the artificial grammar. In the salient condition, the letter strings were organised in columns so that each column represented one underlying stimulus type (grammatical rule). In the non-salient condition the letter strings were shown randomly. After observing the letter strings, the subjects were shown new strings and asked to identify those that were grammatically correct.

The learning modes can be induced relatively easily by external factors. In Reber's research, a learning mode could be induced in the subjects by means of the instructions. If subjects were told to search for rules in an artificial language, they would learn in an explicit mode. If the subjects were led to believe that there were no rules governing the stimulus, they would learn in an implicit mode. Instructions to search for rules that underlay less salient stimulus material had a detrimental impact on the subjects' ability to learn about the structure. Explicit search for rules produced a strong tendency for subjects to induce or invent rules, which were not accurate representations of the stimulus structure. Subjects who, by instruction, were induced to learn in an implicit mode were able to memorise exemplars of the stimulus structure better.

According to the theory, the ideal combination of problem saliency and learning mode would be to learn in an explicit mode if the problem is salient and to learn in an implicit mode if the problem is not salient. The implication of these findings is that people should be induced to learn in a mode that corresponds to the problem saliency. Clearly, this theory is highly relevant for HCI design if it can be shown that different user-interfaces can induce the two learning modes.

Information Modes in HCI

Different information modes are determined by the user-interface. In HCI the user-interface can be defined as "the parts of the system with which the user comes into contact physically, perceptually or cognitively." Consequently, the user-interface includes the hardware (e.g. keyboard, mouse, joy-stick, touch screen), as well as software features (i.e. the graphical and structural organisation of a program).

Tools and Learning Modes

Various interaction tools can induce different learning modes. Some interaction tools require the user to interact directly with the objects of interest (e.g. by directly controlling graphical objects with a mouse). Other interaction tools demand that the user interact by intermediary actions, e.g. by typing commands. The users can "grasp" the virtual objects, which are projected on a normal desktop surface, with a brick.

When the cognitive impact of two given interaction tools differs enough, different learning modes can be induced. Recent research shows that a user interface radically can influence the way people learn by means of a computer. An interaction tool, which induces a learning mode, also has consequences for the learning performance. For example, interaction tools that increase the cognitive load on students when learning (e.g. by demanding the users type commands in order to interact), can induce an explicit learning style.

Interaction tools implying little cognitive load on the users, such as interaction by direct manipulation with graphical objects, tend to induce a more implicit, trial and error learning mode. The success of learning a certain task is closely linked to the chosen learning strategy, due to some strategies being more powerful than others (e.g. the success of implicit and explicit learning modes depends on the task saliency). Consequently, the interaction tool can play a major role in successful learning by supporting or inhibiting certain strategies.

Navigation Methods and Learning Modes

CAL applications demand several kinds of user navigation methods. The navigation strategy is to some extent defined by the characteristics of the learning system. There are many methods of moving between different states, pages or masks in a program. The program can apply one or more methods, and this will have an impact on how the information will be perceived. The navigation strategy also influences the knowledge acquisition, depending on whether an implicit or an explicit navigation strategy can be induced by the navigation tool.

Navigation in a free structured system (e.g. hypertext) can support an implicit learning strategy, because the structure supports spontaneous and unstructured movements (and also because such systems often are highly unsalient). Browsing is an example of an implicit navigation strategy. The hypertext/media based structure of Internet supports navigation by browsing. Browsing is a way of seeking new information; the information can be unknown, but anticipated. Browsing is a member of a set of information seeking activities, or strategies, best suited to covering a large and complex area without going into too much detail. Browsing has associative activities of exploring, scanning and extending. The purpose of browsing may be quite implicit or tacit in the understanding of the searcher.

Simulations are similar to hypertext/media systems in that there is no pre-defined structure of the action sequences. Simulations that incorporate spatial movements, e.g. between rooms in a virtual building, must implement navigation methods and tools, which enable users to walk around. However, because many simulations are characterised by a more tacit change of states depending on the user actions, the aspects of navigation are different from browsing. Hence, operating a simulation is neither browsing nor non-browsing. In simulations demonstrating complex relationships, navigation becomes a matter of selecting the right cognitive strategy for the optimal sequence of actions. The knowledge discovery comes gradually by induction, where in hypermedia systems the knowledge may be explicitly presented on one node.

Simulations that incorporate spatial movements, e.g. between rooms in a virtual building, must implement navigation methods and tools, which enable users to walk around. Non-browsing is more purposeful and focused than browsing. It is more concerned with having a model of what might be possible and exploring options to see which meets chosen criteria. One example is navigation in a structured environment, when people move linearly between pages in a computer-based training program (CBT).

Most computer-based training applications support non-browsing navigation. In such environments the navigation is supported by a structured system. The students are supposed to navigate through the learning material in a structured way; for example, buttons bring the user pages forward or backwards. This kind of navigation was typical for Hypercard applications. Non-browsing strategies can also be employed in a hypertext/media system by users who apply an explicit search strategy to consider the search activities consciously. This can be achieved by purposeful use of available navigation aids like histories or guided tours. Such navigation aids can serve as cognitive tools, i.e. by helping users to follow a structured search strategy.

Visual feedback can be direct or indirect. Direct visual feedback occurs when an action immediately causes a reaction of the program: e.g. a window opens by starting a program, or the scroll bar in a text window scrolls the text. Visual feedback is one of the most powerful effects in simulation-based learning. Interactive simulations can give continuous visual feedback about the effects of different actions in the system. Interaction with graphical interfaces by direct manipulation implies continuous visual feedback about the location and state of objects. This feedback contains indirect information that supports continuous reflections of the ongoing actions. The students interpret the new states of the simulation based on their actions; hence, a series of actions (conscious and purposely or implicit and intuitively) can follow.

With increasing processing power, continuous feedback to the user is appealing. Two actual examples from commercial software illustrate different forms of subtle feedback. The two examples represent continuous and discontinuous methods of feedback respectively: A graphics editor, such as Adobe Photoshop, offers filtering options, which are operated by dialogue boxes. In the dialogue box, different parameters can be changed interactively by moving small handlers on a bar. The effect of a change can often be seen instantly in a small preview box. This gives the user an immediate impression of the effect of such a change.

The use of 3D programs often involves the following situation: when rotating a three-dimensional object, the user is actually manipulating a simple copy of the object, i.e. a 'bounding box'. The object rotated to the new position is not shown until the rotation is finished. From a pedagogical point of view, different feedback content represents an important feature of a CAL system. Verbal forms of feedback communicate direct messages and are, therefore, closely linked to content feedback. Response feedback provides an evaluation of the appropriateness of an action. Approach feedback relates to the chosen task solving strategy. It is realistic for simple tasks with few parameters. It is more complex to design approach feedback for complex tasks.

Motivation feedback is intended to increase the effort put into learning. Source of motivation is an individual matter; thus, many factors may have an influence. It is important to analyse carefully what motivates the target group of a learning program before deciding what to implement. Many effects can serve as cognitive feedback depending on the teaching strategy. Cognitive feedback is involved in all interactions with a system in which the students can observe the consequences of their own actions. In particular visual feedback in simulations can have great impact on the learning performance, by either explicitly or implicitly contributing to knowledge acquisition. Simulation promotes much indirect cognitive feedback; in fact, the idea is not based on instruction, but on letting the students implicitly unveil the learning goals.

ENGLISH TEACHERS' BARRIERS TO THE USE OF COMPUTER-ASSISTED LANGUAGE LEARNING

Computers have been used for language teaching ever since the 1960's. This 40-year period can be divided into three main stages: behaviorist CALL, communicative CALL, and integrative CALL. Each stage corresponds to a certain level of technology and certain pedagogical theories. The reasons for using Computer-assisted Language Learning include:

— experiential learning,

— motivation,

— enhance student achievement,

— authentic materials for study,

— greater interaction,

— individualization,

— independence from a single source of information, and

— global understanding.

The barriers inhibiting the practice of Computer-assisted Language Learning can be classified in the following common categories:

— financial barriers,

— availability of computer hardware and software,

— technical and theoretical knowledge, and

— acceptance of the technology.

In the last few years the number of teachers using Computer-assisted Language Learning (CALL) has increased markedly and numerous articles have been written about the role of technology in education in the 21st century. Although the potential of the Internet for educational use has not been fully explored yet and the average school still makes limited use of computers, it is obvious that we have entered a new information age in which the links between technology and TEFL have already been established.

In the early 90's education started being affected by the introduction of word processors in schools, colleges and universities. This mainly had to do with written assignments. The development of the Internet brought about a revolution in the teachers' perspective, as the teaching tools offered through the Internet were gradually becoming more reliable. Nowadays, the Internet is gaining immense popularity in foreign language teaching and more and more educators and learners are embracing it.

The History of CALL

Computers have been used for language teaching ever since the 1960's. According to Warschauer & Healey, this 40-year period can be divided into three main stages: behaviorist CALL, communicative CALL, and integrative CALL. Each stage corresponds to a certain level of technology and certain pedagogical theories.

Behaviorist CALL

In the 1960's and 1970's the first form of computer-assisted Language Learning featured repetitive language drills, the so-called drill-and-practice method. It was based on the behaviorist learning model and as such the computer was viewed as little more than a mechanical tutor that never grew tired. Behaviorist CALL was first designed and implemented in the era of the mainframe and the best-known tutorial system, PLATO, ran on its own special hardware. It was mainly used for extensive drills, explicit grammar instruction, and translation tests.

Communicative CALL

Communicative CALL emerged in the 1970's and 1980's as a reaction to the behaviorist approach to language learning. Proponents of communicative CALL rejected behaviorist approaches at both the theoretical and pedagogical level. They stressed that CALL should focus more on using forms rather than on the forms themselves. Grammar should be taught implicitly and students should be encouraged to generate original utterances instead of manipulating prefabricated forms. This form of computer-based instruction corresponded to cognitive theories which recognized that learning was a creative process of discovery, expression, and development. The mainframe was replaced by personal computers that allowed greater possibilities for individual work. Popular CALL software in this era included text reconstruction programmers and simulations.

Integrative CALL

The last stage of computer-assisted Language Learning is integrative CALL. Communicative CALL was criticized for using the computer in an ad hoc and disconnected fashion and using the computer made 'a greater contribution to marginal rather than central elements' of language learning. Teachers have moved away from a cognitive view of communicative language teaching to a socio-cognitive view that emphasizes real language use in a meaningful, authentic context. Integrative CALL seeks both to integrate the various skills of language learning (listening, speaking, writing, and reading) and to integrate technology more fully into language teaching. To this end the multimedia-networked computer provides a range of informational, communicative, and publishing tools that are potentially available to every student.

Research and practice suggest that, appropriately implemented, network-based technology can contribute significantly to:

Experiential Learning

The World Wide Web makes it possible for students to tackle a huge amount of human experience. In such a way, they can learn by doing things themselves. They become the creators not just the receivers of knowledge. As the way information is presented is not linear, users develop thinking skills and choose what to explore.

Computers are most popular among students either because they are associated with fun and games or because they are considered to be fashionable. Student motivation is therefore increased, especially whenever a variety of activities are offered, which make them feel more independent. Network-based instruction can help pupils strengthen their linguistic skills by positively affecting their learning attitude and by helping them build self-instruction strategies and promote their self-confidence. All students can use various resources of authentic reading materials either at school or from their home. Those materials can be accessed 24 hours a day at a relatively low cost.

Random access to Web pages breaks the linear flow of instruction. By sending E-mail and joining newsgroups, EFL students can communicate with people they have never met. They can also interact with their own classmates. Furthermore, some Internet activities give students positive and negative feedback by automatically correcting their on-line exercises.

Shy or inhibited students can be greatly benefited by individualized, student-centered collaborative learning. High fliers can also realize their full potential without preventing their peers from working at their own pace. Although students can still use their books, they are given the chance to escape from canned knowledge and discover thousands of information sources. As a result, their education fulfils the need for interdisciplinary learning in a multicultural world.

A foreign language is studied in a cultural context. In a world where the use of the Internet becomes more and more widespread, an English Language teacher's duty is to facilitate students' access to the web and make them feel citizens of a global classroom, practicing communication on a global level.

There is a wide range of on-line applications which are already available for use in the foreign language class. These include dictionaries and encyclopedias, links for teachers, chat-rooms, pronunciation tutors, grammar and vocabulary quizzes, games and puzzles, literary extracts. The World Wide Web (WWW) is a virtual library of information that can be accessed by any user around the clock. If someone wants to read or listen to the news, for example, there are a number of sources offering the latest news either printed or recorded. The most important newspapers and magazines in the world are available on-line and the same is the case with radio and TV channels.

Another example is communicating with electronic pen friends, something that most students would enjoy. Teachers should explain how it all works and help students find their keypals. Two EFL classes from different countries can arrange to send E-mail regularly to one another. This can be done quite easily thanks to the web sites providing lists of students looking for communication. It is also possible for two or more students to join a chat-room and talk on-line through E-mail.. Another network-based EFL activity could be project writing. By working for a project a pupil can construct knowledge rather that only receive it. Students can work on their own, in groups of two or in larger teams, in order to write an assignment, the size of which may vary according to the objectives set by the instructor.

A variety of sources can be used besides the Internet such as school libraries, encyclopedias, reference books etc. The Internet itself can provide a lot of food for thought. The final outcome of their research can be typed using a word processor. A word processor can be used in writing compositions, in preparing a class newsletter or in producing a school home page. In such a Web page students can publish their project work so that it can reach a wider audience. That makes them feel more responsible for the final product and consequently makes them work more laboriously. The Internet and the rise of computer-mediated communication in particular have reshaped the uses of computers for language learning.

The recent shift to global information-based economies means that students will need to learn how to deal with large amounts of information and have to be able to communicate across languages and cultures. At the same time, the role of the teacher has changed as well. Teachers are not the only source of information any more, but act as facilitators so that students can actively interpret and organize the information they are given, fitting it into prior knowledge. Students have become active participants in learning and are encouraged to be explorers and creators of language rather than passive recipients of it. Integrative CALL stresses these issues and additionally lets learners of a language communicate inexpensively with other learners or native speakers. As such, it combines information processing, communication, use of authentic language, and learner autonomy, all of which are of major importance in current language learning theories.

Teachers' Barriers to the Use of CALL

The barriers inhibiting the practice of Computer-assisted Language Learning can be classified in the following common categories

— financial barriers,

— availability of computer hardware and software,

— technical and theoretical knowledge, and

— acceptance of the technology.

Financial Barriers

Financial barriers are mentioned most frequently in the literature by language education practitioners. They include the cost of hardware, software, maintenance (particular of the most advanced equipment), and extend to some staff development. Froke said, "concerning the money, the challenge was unique because of the nature of the technology." Existing universities policies and procedures for budgeting and accounting were well advanced for classroom instruction. The costs of media were accounted for in the university as a part of the cost of instruction. Though the initial investment in hardware is high, inhibiting institutions' introduction of advance technologies; but Hooper recommends that the cost of computers will be so low that they will be available in most schools and homes in the future.

Lewis et al. indicate three conditions under which Computer-assisted Learning and other technologies can be cost-effectiveness: Computer-assisted Learning costs the same as conventional instruction but ends up with producing higher achievement in the same amount of instructional time, it results in students achieving the same level but in less time. These authors indicate that in examples where costs of using technologies in education are calculated, they are usually understand because the value of factors, such as faculty time and cost of equipment utilization, is ignored. Herschbach argues firmly that new technologies are add-on expenses and will not, in many cases, lower the cost of providing educational services. He stated that that the new technologies probably will not replace the teachers, but will supplement their efforts, as has been the pattern with other technologies.

The technologies will not decrease educational costs or increase teacher productivity as currently used. Low usage causes the cost barrier. Computers, interactive instruction TV, and other devices are used very few hours of the day, week, or month. Either the number of learners or the amount of time learners apply the technology must be increased substantially to approach the concept of cost-effectiveness. There are other more quick and less expensive ways of reducing costs, no matter how inexpensive the technology being used.

Availability of Computer Hardware and Software

The most significant aspects of computer are hardware and software. Availability of high quality software is the most pressing challenge in applying the new technologies in education. Underlying this problem is a lack of knowledge of what elements in software will promote different kinds of learning. There are few educators skilled in designing it because software development is costly and time-consuming. McClelland indicated having sufficient hardware in locations where learners have access to it problematic and is, of course, partly a financial problem. Computer hardware and software compatibility goes on to be a significant problem. Choosing hardware is difficult because of the many choices of systems to be used in delivering education, the delivery of equipment, and the rapid changes in technology.

Technical and Theoretical Knowledge

A lack of technical and theoretical knowledge is another barrier to the use of Computer-assisted Language Learning technology. Not only is there a shortage of knowledge about developing software to promote learning, as shown above, but many instructors do not understand how to use the new technologies. Furthermore, little is known about integrating these new means of learning into an overall plan. In the communication between McClelland and C. Dede, Dede indicated the more powerful technologies, such as artificial intelligence in computers, might promote learning of higher-order cognitive skills that are difficult to access with today's evaluation procedures and, therefore, the resulting pedagogical gains may be under-valued. Improper use of technologies can affect both the teacher and learner negatively.

We live in a time change. Gelatt stated that change itself has changed. Change has become so rapid, so turbulent, and so unpredictable that is now called "white water" change. Murphy & Terry indicated the current of change move so quickly that they destroy what was considered the norm in the past, and by doing so, create new opportunities. But, there is a natural tendency for organizations to resist change. Wrong conceptions about the use of technology limit innovation and threaten teachers' job and security. Instructors are tend not to use technologies that require substantially more preparation time, and it is tough to provide instructors and learners access to technologies that are easy to use.

Engaging in Computer-assisted Language Learning is a continuing challenge that requires time and commitment. As we approach the 21st century, we realize that technology as such is not the answer to all our problems. What really matters is how we use technology. Computers can/will never substitute teachers but they offer new opportunities for better language practice. They may actually make the process of language learning significantly richer and play a key role in the reform of a country's educational system. The next generation of students will feel a lot more confident with information technology than we do. As a result, they will also be able to use the Internet to communicate more effectively, practice language skills more thoroughly and solve language learning problems more easily.

4

USING MS WORD FOR LEARNING

OPENING MS WORD

Double click the MS Word icon. The flashing line (insertion point) indicates where the test you type will appear. The top toolbars contain buttons which help you quickly select commonly used commands. The ruler allows you to change margin settings. At the bottom of the screen is the status bar, which contains information about the area of the document displayed on your screen.

ENTERING TEXT

To start a new paragraph, press enter twice on the keyboard. When you reach the end of the line the text will automatically wrap to the next line. You only need to press enter when you want to start a new line or paragraph. Word automatically underlines misspelled words in red and grammar mistakes in green. The red and green will not appear when the document is printed. To correct an error, move the mouse over the error and then press the right mouse button. A menu appears with suggestions to correct the error.

SELECT TEXT

To make any changes in the text appearance, you must first highlight the text by clicking and dragging the mouse over it.

1. To select a word, double click on it with the mouse.
2. To select a sentence, press Ctrl on the keyboard and hold it down while you click the mouse anywhere within the sentence.
3. To select a paragraph move the mouse anywhere over the paragraph you want to select and then quickly press the left mouse button three times.

Once text has been selected you can change the style, size, alignment, or appearance.

EDITING TEXT

Insert Text

1. Click the mouse where you want to insert the new text.
2. Type the text you wish to insert.

Insert Blank Line

1. Click the mouse where you want to insert the blank line.
2. Press enter to insert a blank line.

Delete text

1. Click the mouse to the right of the first character you wish to delete. Press Backspace on the keyboard to delete.

   Or

2. Click the mouse to the right of the first character you wish to delete. Press Delete on the keyboard to delete.

Delete a blank line

1. Click the mouse at the beginning of the line you wish to delete and press backspace to remove it.

Delete selected text

1. Select text (click and drag mouse).
2. Press Delete on keyboard.

Undo last change

1. Click Edit, Undo

Or

2. Click the Undo button beside the globe on the standard toolbar.

Move text

1. Select text (click and drag mouse).
2. Move the mouse over the selected text until it becomes an arrow.
3. Press and hold down the left mouse button as you move the mouse to the desired location.
4. Release the mouse and the text will appear in the new location.
5. To undo press the undo button on the standard toolbar.

   Or

1. Select text (click and drag mouse).
2. Move the mouse over the scissors (cut) button on the standard toolbar.
3. Move the mouse to the new location for the text.
4. Move the mouse to the paste button (beside the broom) on the standard toolbar.

Copying text

1. Select text (click and drag mouse).

2. Press and hold Ctrl on keyboard.
3. Continue holding down Ctrl as you click and drag the mouse to the location you wish to copy the text.
4. Release the Ctrl key and the left mouse button.

   Or

1. Select text (click and drag mouse).
2. Move the mouse to the copy button on the standard toolbar (beside the scissors).
3. Move the mouse to the new location for the text and click.
4. Press the Paste button on the standard toolbar (beside the broom).

This feature helps you find a word or phrase in your document.

1. Click Edit.
2. Click Find.
3. Type the word you wish to find in the Find and Replace dialog box.
4. Click Find Next in the dialog box.
5. Word highlights the first match, click Find Next to find the next time the word appears.

Replace Text

1. Click Edit.
2. Click Replace.
3. In the dialog box type the word you wish to find and the replacement word.

CHECK SPELLING AND GRAMMAR

Word underlines misspelled words in red and grammar mistakes in green. To correct an error:

1. Move the mouse over the error.
2. Click the right mouse button.
3. Make your choice from the menu suggestions to correct the error.

Ignore an error

1. Move the mouse over the error and press the right mouse button.
2. Click Ignore All or Ignore Sentence.

When you finish typing your document, you can find and correct all selling and grammar errors at once.

Correct Entire Document

Click the Spell and Grammar Check button on the standard toolbar (ABC with check). Errors will appear in the dialog box and give you the option to Ignore or change the word.

USING THE THESAURUS

The thesaurus replaces a word with one that is more suitable.

1. Click the word you wish to replace.
2. Click Tools.
3. Move the mouse to Language.
4. Click Thesaurus.
5. The Thesaurus dialog box appears and gives you the opportunity to select a replacement word by clicking the word of your choice and then click Replace.

USING AUTO CORRECT

Word automatically corrects hundreds of common typing, spelling, and grammar errors.

1. Highlight passage (click and drag mouse).
2. Click Tools.
3. Click Auto Correct.

Once an entry is corrected, Auto Correct will automatically insert the correct entry each time it appears in the document. It will correct errors you commonly make in words and phrases that you frequently use.

USING AUTO TEXT

To avoid typing the same text over and over again, you can store text you frequently use in Auto Text.

1. Type and highlight the text you wish to store.
2. Move the mouse to Insert.
3. Move the mouse to Auto Text and click New.
4. The Auto Text dialog box appears.
5. Type a name for the entry and click OK.

You have now created an Auto Text entry. To insert it follow these directions:

1. Click the mouse where you want the entry to appear.
2. Move the mouse to Insert, Auto Text and in the next column Normal.
3. Click the name of the entry you wish to insert.

COUNTING WORDS IN A DOCUMENT

To determine the number of words in a document:

1. Move the mouse to Tools, Word Count and click.
2. A dialog box appears that displays information about the document.

FORMATTING TEXT

Bold, Italic, Underline

1. Highlight desired text.
2. Click one of these buttons on the Formatting Toolbar: B (Bold), I (Italics), or U(underline).
3. The text you selected will appear in the new style.

Alignment of Text

1. Highlight the desired text.
2. Select an alignment button from the Formatting Toolbar (Align left, Align center, Align right, Justify.
3. The text you selected will appear in the new alignment.

Changing Font Style or Size

1. Highlight desired text.
2. Click the down arrow beside the words: Times New Roman on the Formatting Toolbar and select the desired font style.
3. Click the down arrow beside the number 12 on the Formatting Toolbar and select the desired font size.

Changing Font Color

1. Highlight desired text.
2. At the right end of the Formatting Toolbar click the down arrow beside the letter A and select the desired font color.

Highlight Text Feature

1. Highlight desired text.
2. At the right end of the Formatting Toolbar click the down arrow beside the Highlight pen.

3. Select the desired highlight color.
4. The desired text will appear highlighted in the color you selected.

Changing Appearance of Text

1. Highlight desired text.
2. Click Format.
3. Click Font
4. In the Font dialog box, click the Font tab and select a design for your highlighted text and click. You can change the font, font style, size, color, and effects.

Inserting Symbols @

1. Click the mouse where you want the symbol inserted in your document.
2. Click Insert, Symbol.
3. In the Symbol dialog box select Font: Symbol.
4. Click the symbol you wish to insert and then click, Insert.
5. Click Close.

Adding Bullets or Numbers

1. Highlight the text you wish to have bullets or numbers displayed.
2. Click Format
3. Click Bullets and Numbering
4. In the Bullets and Numbering dialog box click the type of list you want to create.
5. Click the style you desire.
6. Click Ok.

To add bullets or numbers as you type:

1. Click the mouse where you want the first number or bullet.
2. Type 1. followed by a space (if you desire numbered list)
3. Type * followed by a space if you want a bulleted list.

When you press enter for the next line a bullet or number will automatically appear.

Add a Border

1. Highlight the area you want display a border.
2. Click the Tables and Borders button on the Standard Toolbar beside the Globes.
3. Select a line style, thickness, and type of border in this dialog box.

Add Shading

1. Highlight the area you want shaded.
2. Click the Tables and Borders button on the Standard Toolbar beside the Globes.
3. To select a shaded color, click the last button in the dialog box.
4. The shading will appear.

Selecting Line Spacing

1. Highlight the paragraphs you wish to change to a new line spacing.
2. Click Format, Paragraph.
3. In the Paragraph dialog box click Indents and Spacing tab.
4. Select the line spacing you desire and click.

Indenting Paragraphs

1. On the left top ruler line are symbols that let you indent the left edge of a paragraph.

Indent first line

Indent all but first line

Indent all lines

2. Highlight the paragraph you wish to indent.

3. Click the indent symbol and drag it to the desire position. A line will show you the new indent position.

4. Release the mouse button and Word will indent the paragraph you selected.

   There are two buttons on the Formatting Toolbar to help you quickly indent a paragraph

   Decrease Indent and Increase Indent buttons.

Changing Tab Settings

Word offers four types of tabs:

1. Left Tab
2. Right Tab
3. Center Tab
4. Decimal Tab

Adding a Tab

1. If the ruler is not on screen, click View, and check Ruler.

2. Highlight text you want to contain new tab. To add tab to text you are about to type, move the mouse to where you want to type the text and click.

3. Move the mouse over the button to the left of the ruler. Click the button until the type of tab you want to add appears:

   Left Tab

   Center Tab

Right Tab

Decimal Tab

4. Click and drag the mouse to the bottom half of the ruler to where you want to add the tab.To use a tab, click the mouse at the beginning of the line you want to move across then press Tab on your keyboard and the cursor moves to the first tab.

To move a tab:

1. Highlight the text containing the tab you want to move.
2. On the top ruler click and drag the mouse button as you move the tab to a new position on the ruler.
3. When the mouse button is released, the text will move to the new position.

To remove a tab:

1. Highlight the text containing the tab you want to remove.
2. Click and drag the tab on the top ruler moving the tab downward off the ruler.
3. Release the mouse button and the tab disappears from the ruler.

Copy Formatting

You may want to copy the formatting of text to make all the headings or important words in your document look the same. This will give the document a consistent appearance.

1. Highlight the text that displays the formatting you want to copy.
2. On the Standard Toolbar click the Format Painter button (resembles a paintbrush).
3. The mouse will take on the image of the brush.
4. Highlight the text you want to display the same formatting.

5. Release the mouse button and the text will display the formatting.

Adding Page Numbers

1. Display your document in the Page Layout view by clicking View, Page Layout.
2. Click Insert, Page Numbers.
3. In the dialog box, select the location of the page number, the alignment, and check to show the number on the first page.

Adding Headers and Footers

1. Display your document in the Page Layout view by clicking View, Page Layout.
2. Click View, Header and Footer.
3. Type the header in the text box and format as you would any other text.
4. To create a footer, click the Switch Between Header and Footer button in the Header and Footer toolbar.

Inserting A Page Break

1. Click the mouse where you want to start a new page.
2. Click Insert, Break.
3. In the Break dialog box, click OK.

You can also insert a section break using the same procedure. In the Break dialog box choose one of the following options:

— Next page-Creates a new section on a new page.

— Continuous-Creates a new section on the current page

— Centering Text on a Page

You can vertically center text on a page. This is useful for creating title pages or short memos.

1. Highlight the area you want centered and click.
2. Click File, Page Setup.
3. In the Page Setup dialog box, click the Layout tab and select the Vertical Text Alignment.
4. Click OK.

Changing Margins

1. Click the Print Preview button on the toolbar (beside the printer).
2. The document will appear in the Print Preview window.
3. Click and drag the mouse over the margin you wish to change on the ruler. If the ruler doesn't display click the view ruler button on the toolbar.
4. A line will appear to show the new location of the margin.

Changing Paper Orientation

1. Click File.
2. Click Page Setup.
3. In the Page Setup dialog box click tabs to change the margins, paper size, paper source, and layout.

Creating Newspaper Columns

1. Display the document in the Page Layout view by selecting View, Page Layout
2. Highlight the text you want to display newspaper columns and click the columns button on the Standard Toolbar.

3. You must then select the number (1, 2, 3, or 4) of columns you wish to create.
4. The text will appear in newspaper columns.

Printing Your Document

1. Before printing you can preview your document by clicking the Print Preview button on the Standard Toolbar (beside the printer icon).You can view multiple pages by using the side scroll bar. You can also zoom by clicking the Magnifier button in the preview toolbar. When you finish your preview click close on the toolbar.
2. To print the document click File, Print. The Print dialog box appears. You may choose the following print options: All-Prints every page of the document.

   Current Page-Prints the page containing the mouse cursor.

   Pages-Prints the pages you specify.

   Selection-Prints the text you selected.

   If you wish to print an entire document click the Printer icon on the Standard Toolbar.

GRAPHICS

Inserting Shapes

1. Click the Drawing button on the Standard toolbar.
2. At the bottom of your screen a Drawing toolbar will appear. Click Auto Shapes and select the shape you desire.
3. Click the mouse inside your document where you wish to add the shape. The shape can then be resized, moved, or formatted. It can also be filled with a color.

Resizing Graphics

1. Click on the graphic with the mouse and drag a corner to the desired shape.
2. Moving Graphics
3. Click on the graphic. Click and drag the mouse to the desired location.

Recoloring Graphics

1. Display the drawing toolbar by clicking the drawing button on the Standard toolbar.
2. Click the graphic and then click the paint bucket (fill color) in the drawing toolbar.
3. Select the desired color.

Inserting Clipart, Graphics, or Pictures

In the document, click the mouse where you want to add a graphic.

Click Insert at the top of the screen.

Click Picture.Then choose from Clip Art... or From File...

If you are using a Clip Art picture follow these directions:

Select the clip art image you desire and click Insert. The image can then be resized, formatted, or moved on the screen.

If you are using a picture From File click the location of the image and then its name. Click Insert to place the image into the document.The image can then be resized, formatted, or moved on the screen.

To delete an image, click on it with the mouse and press the delete key on the keyboard.

Formatting an Image

1. Right click the mouse on the image.
2. Choose Format Picture.
3. Click the Wrap tab.
4. Click the desired text wrap effect and then click OK.

WORD ART

1. Display the drawing toolbar by clicking the drawing button on the Standard toolbar.
2. On the drawing toolbar at the bottom of your screen, click the Insert Word Art button.
3. Select the word art effect you desire and click.
4. Click OK.
5. The Word Art can then be moved, recolored, resized, or formatted.

SAVE A DOCUMENT

There are several ways to save a document:

1. Click the diskette icon on the toolbar. If this is the time you have saved this document the Save As dialog box will appear. You will need to supply the name of the document, and the location in which you wish to save it. Warning: If you want to save this document under a new name, do not use this process. It will copy this document over the information saved previously under this name.
2. Click File, Save This process works exactly like step 1 above.
3. Click File, Save as... This process will save a previously saved document and give you the opportunity to rename it and save it under a new name.

CLOSING A DOCUMENT

When you finish working with a document you can close it to remove it from your screen using one of these methods:

1. Click File, Close.Word removes the document from you screen. If you had more than one document open, the second last document you worked with would appear.
2. Click the X in the upper right corner of the screen.

EXIT WORD

1. Save all documents before exiting.
2. Click File
3. Click Exit.

OPENING A DOCUMENT

1. Click the open folder icon on the toolbar.
2. Select the drive and folder of the document.
3. Select the name of the document.

Quickly Opening a Document

1. Click File
2. At the bottom of the drop down menu you will see the names of previously saved documents.
3. Double click the document name.

FINDING A DOCUMENT

If you cannot remember the name or location of a document, you can have Word search for the document.

1. Click the open folder icon on the top toolbar.

2. Click the next to last button (Preview button) in the Open dialog box toolbar. This button displays the contents of a highlighted document.

3. To have Word search for a document, click the drive you want to search.

4. To search the contents of all folders in that drive click the last button (commands and settings) in the Open dialog box toolbar.

GETTING HELP

1. To display the Office Assistant, click the ? button in the top right hand corner of the toolbar.
2. Type the question you want to ask and press enter.
3. The Office Assistant will display a list of help topics that relate to the question you asked.
4. Click the help topic information that matches your request.
5. The Help Window will appear and display information about your topic.
6. When you finish reading the information, press the X to close the screen.
7. To hide the Office Assistant, press the X.

CHANGE DOCUMENT DISPLAY

To change the view Click View, Page Layout, and select the view you desire. You can display your document four ways:

1. Normal View

   When you first open your document it will appear in the Normal view. This view simplifies the document so you can quickly enter, edit, and format text.The Normal view does not display top or bottom margins, headers, footers or page numbers.

2. Page Layout View

   This view displays the document as it will appear on a printed page. It displays top and bottom margins, headers, footers and page numbers.

3. Outline View

   This view helps you review and work with the structure of a document. You can focus on the main headings by hiding the remaining text.

4. Online Layout View

   This view displays documents so they are easy to read on the screen. The Online Layout view displays a document map, which lets you, move quickly to a specific location in our document.

Zoom In or Out

To display the zoom settings, move the mouse over the down arrow beside the 100% in the toolbar and select a zoom in or zoom out setting.

Display or Hide Ruler

To display or hide the ruler, click View. A check mark beside ruler tells you the ruler is currently displayed to hide the ruler, remove the check mark by clicking it.

Display or Hide Toolbars

To display or hide toolbars :

1. Click View
2. Move the mouse to Toolbars. a list of toolbars appears.
3. You may select the toolbar you wish.

Standard Toolbar

This toolbar is directly beneath the top row of text. It has quick keys that allow you to open files, print, check spelling, hyperlink, undo, insert graphs and tables, and zoom.

Formatting Toolbar

This toolbar is beneath the Standard Toolbar. The quick keys on this toolbar allow you to format text style, size, appearance, alignment, insert bullets, numbered list, and change text color.

Document Map

A Document Map allows you to move through a document quickly.

1. Click the Document Map button on the Standard toolbar. (This button is at the right end of the Standard Toolbar.)
2. When the Document Map appears on the left side of your document you can instantly jump to a heading in the document by clicking the mouse on the heading you desire.
3. To hide the Document Map display repeat step 1.

USING ADVANCED FEATURES OF MS WORD FOR REVIEWING TOOLS

MS Word has a range of features which allow you to use it in support of ' iterative' data analysis in which you re-read, sort and attempt to develop 'categories' from transcripts, observation notes and interviews. The processes of 'marking up' texts, 'memoing', and sorting data into emerging categoris can be replicated using Word's 'reviewing' tools. You can make these appear by selecting View -> Toolbars -> Reviewing from the Word Menu. Two of these tools - the 'post-it notes' and the 'highlighters' are shown in figure 1. A nice feature allows you to view all the comments you have appended to a document

- rather like footnotes - in addition to seeing them as 'pop-up' boxes as shown in the illustration above. This doesn't work for highlighters, however.

USING THE ADVANCED FEATURES OF MS WORD: ADVANCED SEARCHING

The 'Find' function of Word (Edit -> Find) or 'CTRL + F' on the keyboard allows you to enter words or phrases which will then be highlighted. You can then skip through a document finding all the instances of the target by using the 'Find Next' button. This is useful if you are reviewing transcripts and want to find all the instances where a particular word was used or a particular person spoke (figure 2).

If you select the 'More' button, you will be given more search options. One which is very useful is the use of 'wildcards'. These allow you do run simple 'concordance' searches, so you can find, for example all the occurrences of a word or phrase spoken by a specific person, or of two words occurring in the same paragraph. For example, if you are looking for occurrences of the words 'science' and 'computer' together a search with 'use wildcards' selected for 'science * computer' will be interpreted as 'look for 'science' followed by any number(the *) of characters followed by 'computer'.

Where this really scores is when you only want to search for specific things being said by specific people. For example: 'Interviewee: * science * computer' will allow you to find occurrences of the Interviewee using the selected word but will ignore the same things being said by the Interviewer. This depend on you formatting and labelling transcripts consistently, of course!

SELECTING AND PRESENTING DATA WITHIN YOUR DISSERTATION OR ESSAY

You are probably best off using MS Word as 'framework' within which you collect your data - photographs, sketches, scanned

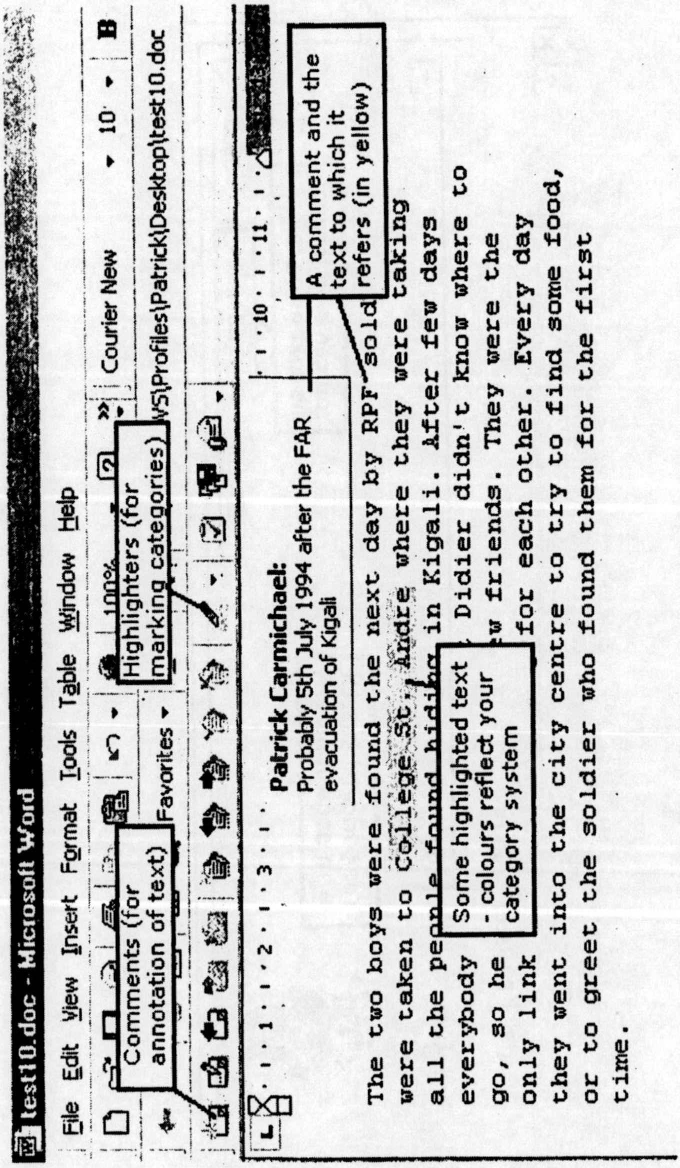

Figure 1: MS Word's Reviewing Tools in Action

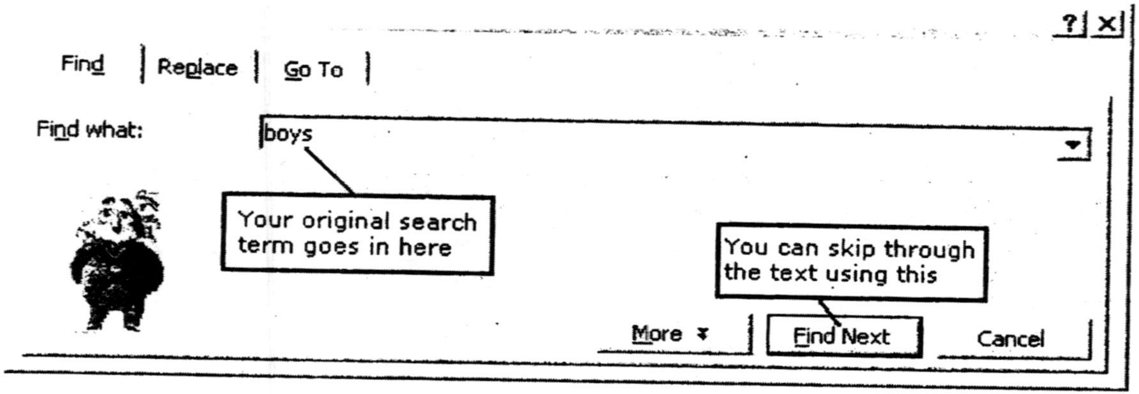

Figure 2: A Search in MS Word

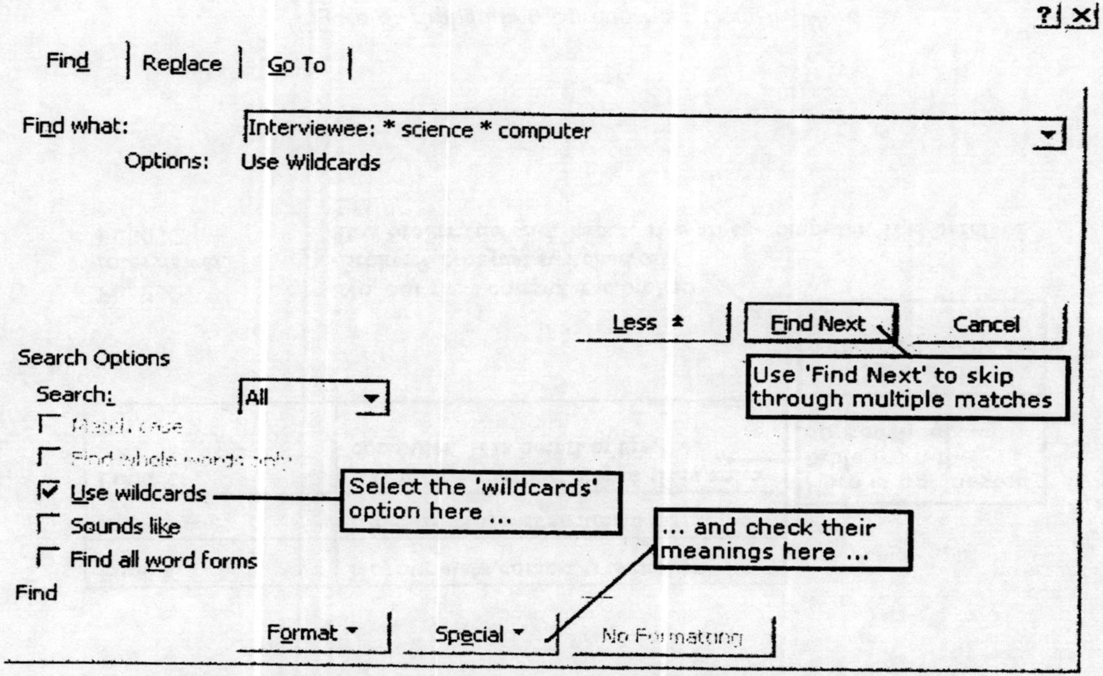

Figure 3: A More Complex Search with 'Wildcards' in MS Word

Pupil X:	No, our class computer is broken
Interviewer:	Broken? Not just switched off?
Pupil X:	It is broken, defunct, kaput. It is an ex-computer. It is bereft of life.

Here is the 'pasted' table from the spreadsheet ...

And here is the converted 'table-to text'

Pupil X: No, our class computer is broken
Interviewer: Broken? Not just switched off?
Pupil X: It is broken, defunct, kaput. It is an ex-computer. It is bereft of life.

Figure 8: Embedding Spreadsheet Data in Word

childrens' work, tables, charts etc can be 'embedded' within your document. Portions of the spreadsheets you may have used for interview data can be 'pasted' into word documents. By default, they will appear as 'tables', so you can then use the table converter (Table -> Convert ->Table to Text) to change them into nicely formatted paragraphs. Remember - never type anything more than once (figure 4)

You don't need to present all your data in the finished essay or dissertation. If there are large data sets it may be worth including them in an appendix, but in the context of most writing, carefully-chosen excerpts, summary tables and charts are probably worth more than page after page of transcripts and multi-coloured three-dimensional exploded pie charts.

USING MS WORD IN E-LEARNING

Using comment boxes to mark and annotate Word documents. If students submit work in Word format, either via floppy disk, intranet or VLE, then a simple way to add comments is by using the 'comments' tag. Do this by highlighting the word, phrase or sentence that you wish to annotate and use 'Insert' and 'Comment' . In windows 2000, when the student runs the mouse over the highlighted area, a 'comment box' will appear. In Windows XP, a comments box appears in the right margin. See the examples below. To revert to the hovering comment box, go to 'Tools' then 'Options' then 'Track changes' and uncheck the balloons box.

If your computer has a sound card and a microphone, you can record 'voice comments' . These are added as sound objects inline with the text.

On the 'toolbar' , click the arrow next to 'New comment' Click 'Voice comment' , and then press the red button and record your comment. This feature could be used to aid pronunciation e.g. when learning languages, or technical terms.

Using hyperlinks in Word

You can link to other documents or to web pages by using 'Insert' and 'Hyperlink' and following the on-screen instructions.

This is a hyperlink to a web page. Note that once a web page has been visited, the computer will 'cache' these pages for a fixed length of time without you saving them. Alternatively, you can click on the 'Organise Favourites' button on the web and click on 'Make available off-line'.

Creating mix and match exercises

Cut and Paste

You can use 'Cut' and 'Paste' to create a mix and match quiz. Students highlight the appropriate text and 'Cut' it. The text can then be placed in the correct box and 'Pasted' in. The example below uses a table.

RSC-YH	The National Learning Network has a variety of online resources for curriculum areas.
JISC	Here to support colleges in the implementation and use of Information and Learning Technology (ILT) into the curriculum.
NLN	A strategic advisory committee working on behalf of the funding bodies for further and higher education (FE and HE) in England, Scotland, Wales and Northern Ireland

Click and Drag

You can create a cloze exercise by placing the missing words in text boxes. The students can then 'Click' onto the words and 'Drag' them into the appropriate gaps.

Mix and Match with scanned images

Using the same principle as above, you can include images in your resources.

Using Forms

You can use 'Forms' to create drop-down boxes, either within a text document or to generate multi-choice questionnaires.

Go to 'View' , then 'Toolbars' , then 'Forms' . Click on this and you will see the 'Forms' toolbar (see above).

To put in a multi-choice form, highlight the word or phrase, then click onto 'Drop down form field' button. (Hover the mouse over the buttons in the box to familiarize yourself with their different functions).

Alternatively, if you want to insert a form at the end of a piece of text, you can simply click onto the onto 'Drop down form field' button and a blank box will appear.

Next click onto the next button, 'Form field options' . This is where you insert the optional words or phrases. A good tip is to insert a row of spaces in the first line, as this will show a blank box in the text, with a drop-down arrow to access the options.

After you have finished, click onto the 'Padlock' . This will lock the document. Once the form is locked, the drop-down boxes can be accessed, the answer can be selected and then the document can be either printed off or saved to disk.

Using other 'Forms' functions

Go to 'View' , then 'Toolbars' , then 'Forms' . Click on this and you will see the 'Forms' toolbar. You can produce tests which require the student to type in the answer by typing a question and then clicking on the 'Text form field' box. This will produce a ' greyed out' box which, when the form is locked, will be the only part of the page that can be modified. This is particularly useful for producing on-line tests.

You can generate tests or forms which require a yes/no answer in a similar way by clicking on the 'Check box form field' option and then locking the page in the normal way.

Using colours and watermarks

Go to "Format" , then "Background". You can change the colour of the background (useful for dyslexic students) or insert a pattern, picture or text message as a watermark.

Using the Picture toolbar

Go to "View", then "Toolbars" then "Picture" - click on the box and the toolbar will appear. Using this toolbar you can insert pictures . Images can be found on Google Image search, saved into a folder and inserted from here, You can alter the properties of the image using the "color" button.You can crop a picture using the "crop" button.

If you right click on the picture and go down to "Format Picture", you can decide on the layout, whether the image is tight with the text, square with the text, whether it overlies it or is overlain by the text.

5

USING MS EXCEL FOR LEARNING

TOOLS AND FEATURES OF EXCEL'S

Application Window

When you load Excel, you may see a "Tip of the Day" screen appear. (On new installations this will appear, but the display is often turned off.) Click on the "OK" button to close the tip screen and go on to the Excel screen. You should see the application window at the top of the screen and a document window below. You can maximize both of these windows, if you want.

The application window area contains five rows or lines of command menus which can be used to act upon the information found in the document window. These command menus display command words and graphic icons. These menus include the *title bar* followed by the *menu bar*, the *Standard toolbar*, the *Formatting toolbar*, the *Formula bar*, and the *Status bar*. The function of each of these is as follows:

Title Bar

Displays the name of the application "Microsoft Excel." The control menu box is on the far left and the minimize/maximize or restore buttons on the far right. These are standard Windows features, and you can consult the Windows manual for additional information.

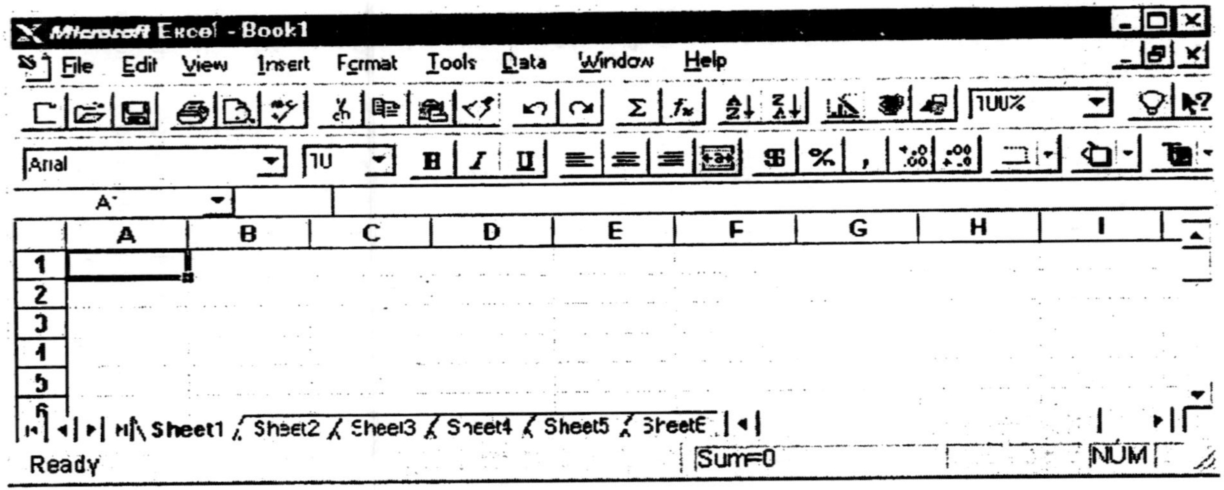

Figure 1. Application Window of MS Excel

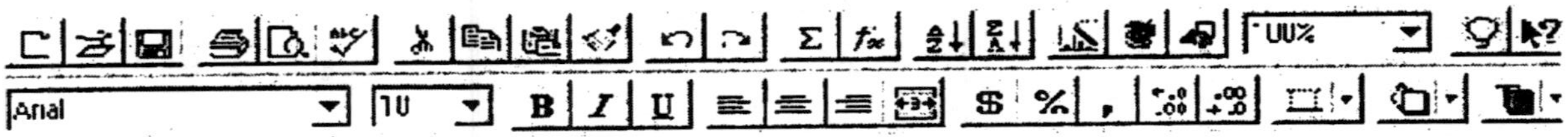

Figure 2. Toolbars of MS Excel

Menu Bar

Displays the main level commands. These commands can be executed with a click of the left mouse button; then additional command options are presented in pull-down menus. The commands FILE, EDIT, VIEW, WINDOW and HELP are common menu options found in other Windows applications.

Toolbars

There are two toolbars which normally display—the Standard toolbar and the Formatting toolbar. The toolbars have graphic icon buttons which can be mouse clicked to perform an action or bring up another set of menus. The actions performed by the toolbar buttons are also found in the menu bar/pull-down menus. Buttons are popular with Excel users because they give a quick way to perform an action but it is not NECESSARY to use them. Because the buttons duplicate menu items, there are often several ways to "perform an action." If you put your mouse pointer on top of a button, its *ToolTip* (name) will pop up. If two toolbars are not displaying, click on VIEW on the menu bar, then Toolbars. A list of the toolbars appears. Click on the box in front of the toolbar name to display it.

Some toolbar buttons are given below:

 New Workbook (results in a blank document)

 Open (workbook/file)

 Save (workbook/file)

 Print

 AutoSum (to add up numbers in a row or column)

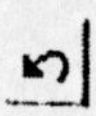 Undo (un-does the last editing action)

Formula Bar

This is the last line before the document window. It displays information entered or about to be entered in a cell and gives the address location of that cell. Cell editing can also be done on this formula bar. The active cell position is indicated on the far left end of the Formula bar ... more about this later.

Status Bar

Displays information about the current state of the program. This feature is located at the very bottom of the document window. The user is provided information about what Excel is doing. Examples are Ready when Excel will accept new entries or Edit if you are editing a cell.

TOOLS AND FEATURES OF EXCEL'S

Document/Workbook Window

Just below the application window is the document or workbook window.

This is the window where the spreadsheet information will appear. If this window is not maximized, the top of this window also contains a document title bar which will display the filename. Below the title bar is a grid matrix area where information will be displayed or entered. There is a vertical scroll bar on the right margin, a horizontal scroll bar at the bottom right, and sheet tab controls at the bottom left. Each of these items is listed and described below.

Title Bar

This will only appear if the document window is not maximized. It displays the workbook (file) name. The name on a blank application would be Book1, Book2, etc., depending on how many windows are open. You can click on this title bar and drag it to move the window. The control menu box is at the left end and the minimize and maximize buttons are on the right end. (The minimize and maximize buttons look different on Windows 3.1.)

Workbook Page

Contains the grid matrix of cells (defined below) where the spreadsheet information will be entered or found. The column headings are referenced by alphabetic characters and the rows are referenced by numbers found on the left. The area where the column letters and row numbers are found is called the frame.

Scroll Bars

The scroll bars are used to view different parts of the spreadsheet. You use the vertical scroll bar at the right margin to move vertically or the horizontal scroll bar at the bottom right to move horizontally.

Sheet Tabs and Scrolling Buttons

Tabs appear at the bottom of the document window with names of Sheet1, Sheet2, Sheet3, etc. (Refer to the diagram above.) You can go to another sheet by clicking on a different tab. Also, the scrolling buttons appear to the left of the tabs; they allow you to scroll more quickly through the sheets.

LEARNING EXCEL: BASIC TERMS AND DEFINITIONS

These are additional terms you need to. know:

Cell

This is the basic unit of the spreadsheet. It is a location that can contain information and is most often defined by its column and row address. For example C6 represents a cell in the third column (column C) and sixth row. The naming convention for a cell reference is the alphabetic column letter position followed by the row number. C6 is correct but 6C is incorrect. You may use either lower or upper case letters when referencing a column.

Active Cell or Selected Cell

The cell which has the dark border around it is the *active cell.* This is the cell that can be acted upon and indicates where the insertion point is located. You can select a new active cell by using the keyboard's arrow keys or clicking on a new cell with the mouse. You can also use keys like [PageDown] and [PageUp] and [Home] to change the active cell location.

Block

A group of adjacent cells forming a rectangle is called a block. It is defined by the addresses of the two cells that are in the opposite corners of the rectangle block area, from the top left cell in the block to the bottom right cell in the block. A block of cells can be marked by using the mouse or by holding down the shift key and using the arrow keys. Once a block is defined, you can do many things with that block such as move it, copy it, delete it, or alter the display of its contents with formatting options.

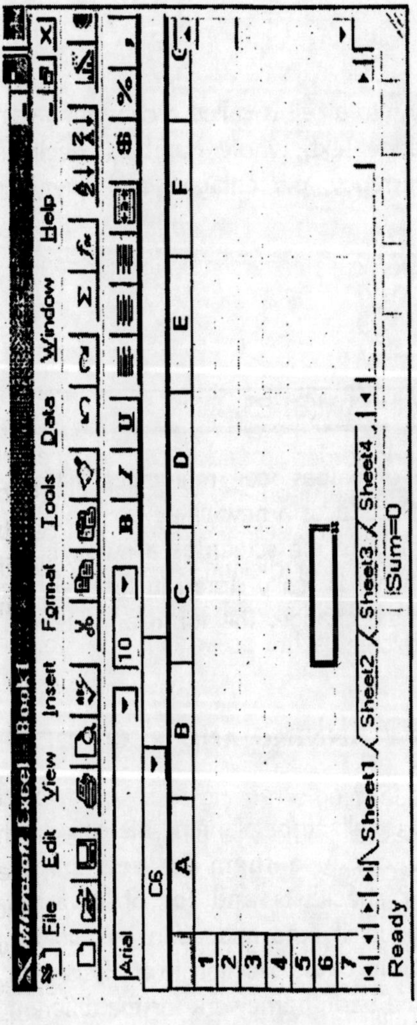

Figure 3. Cell of MS Excel

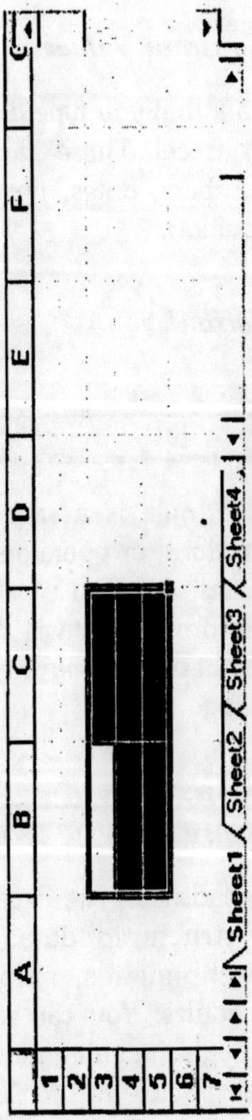

Figure 4. Cell of MS Excel

Workbook

This is Excel's name for a file. The workbook can have multiple sheets with different information on each sheet. This permits you to keep related data in one file rather than break it up into several different files.

Constant Values

Data that you type directly into a cell is called a constant value by Excel. These can include text, whole numbers, decimal numbers, dates, times, currency, percentages, and scientific notation.

Formulas

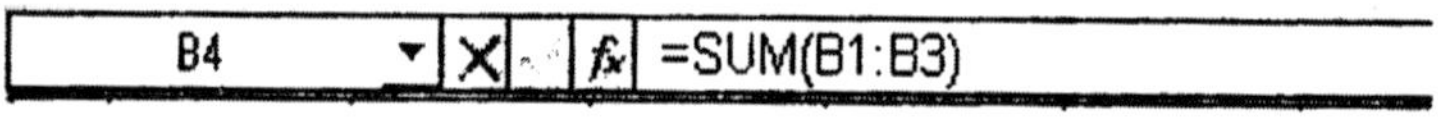

A formula is a sequence of values, cell references, names, functions, or operators that produces a new value from existing values. A formula will display on the screen as a number but the formula bar will show what is really stored in that cell. As numbers affecting the formula change, the formula value will change.

USING MS EXCEL FOR PLANNING AND RECORDING SEQUENCES OF EVENTS

Spreadsheets like Excel are excellent for planning the collection of structured data. You can use them for setting out questionnaires, preparing checklists and for observation schedules. You can save yourself time and effort by thinking through the entire process from data collection to analysis: you may be able to use the same basic framework for the different processes. Here is a simple example for collecting, storing and analysing structured interview data.

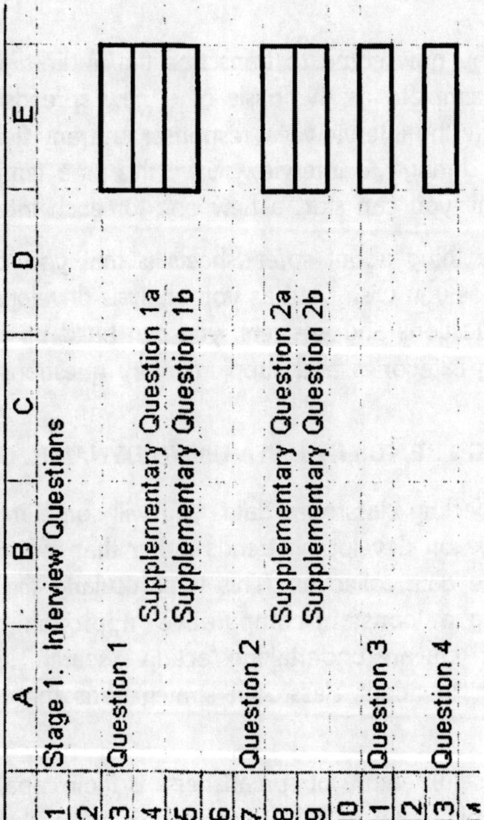

Figure 5. Setting out a Questionnaire Schedule in MS Excel

First, you can write up your questionaire schedule and save it as a 'document template' - you'll be needing it again later! Print out as many copies as have interviewees and then use them to keep track of which questions you asked and they answered. This will provide a useful way of cross-checking with audio-tapes. You may want to jot down notes on the sheet as well.

When you now come to transcribe the audio-tapes, you can use the template as the basis of a new spreadsheet on which to collate the interviewees' responses and any field notes you collected during the interview. Save this as a template as well - that way you can start a new one for each interview.

The nice thing about spreadsheets is that you can add new columns as you wish, and as you analysis develops. So in addition to questions and answers, you can build up columns with emerging categories and supplementary questions.

MONITORING TRENDS IN DATA USING DYNAMIC CHARTS

If you are collecting classroom data, you will sometimes want to keep an eye on developing trends rather than waiting until the end of the data collection. This is particularly the case if you are using a 'constant-comparative' approach to your research, or if you are undertaking 'action research' in which you may wish to adapt classroom strategies as the research develops.

A very useful feature of spreadsheets is their capability to present 'dynamic' data; in MS Windows this is also known as OLE or 'Object Linking and Embedding'. Here is a simple example. Let us assume that you are counting the number of undirected teacher questions answered by boys and girls - you might be using some kind of observation schedule. You set up a spreadsheet as shown below, and, even though you haven't collected all your data yet, plot a chart to show differences - but making sure the the 'chart area' which you select includes

	A	B	C	D	E
1	Stage 2:	Interview Responses			
2					
3	Name:	Blair, Tony		Date:	April 1997
4					
5	Question 1				Education, education education
6		Supplementary Question 1a			Well, it depends on what you mean by
7		Supplementary Question 1b			I wish!
8					
9	Question 2				Not as far as I'm aware
10		Supplementary Question 2a			
11		Supplementary Question 2b			
12					
13	Question 3				No (inaudible)
14					
15	Question 4				Alistair? Do we have a policy on this?

Figure 6. Questionnaire Data in MS Excel

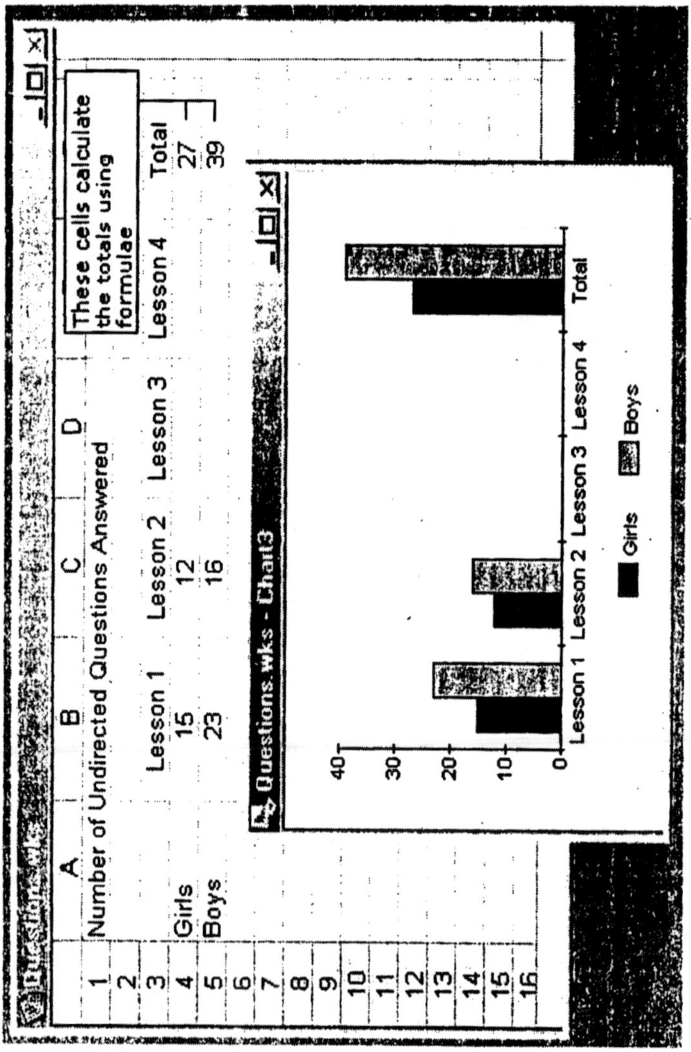

Figure 7. Charting Spreadsheet Data (1)

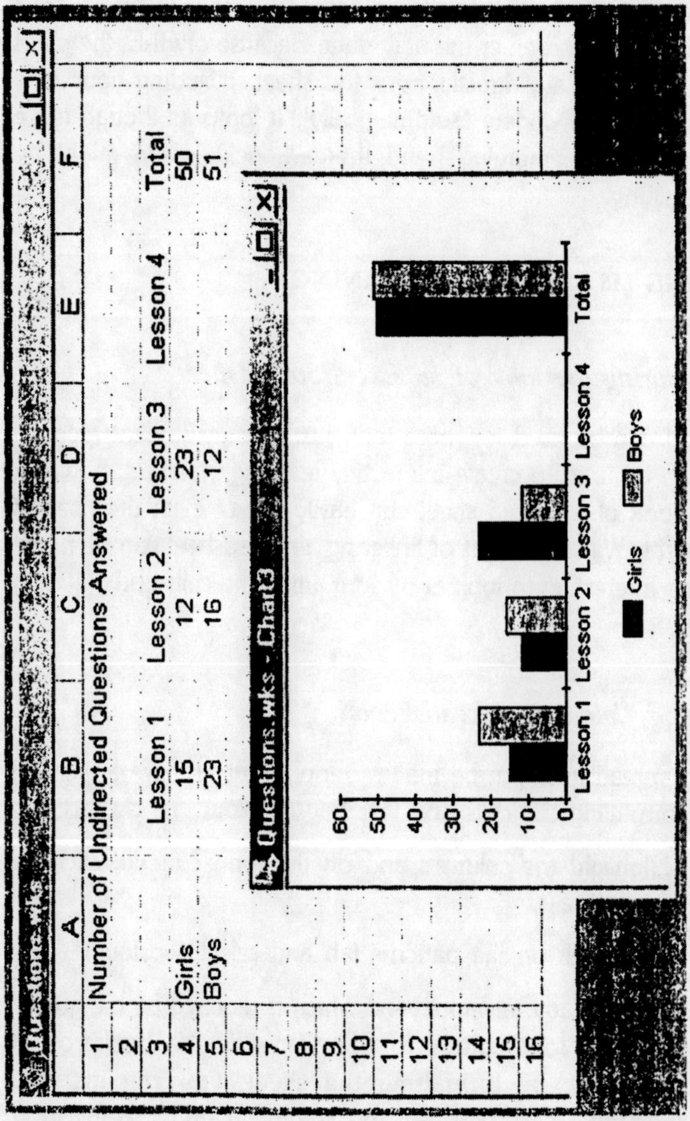

Figure 8. Charting Spreadsheet Data (2)

the blanks you intend to fill in later. Then you save the sheet and the chart.

After another visit to the classroom, you re-open your spreadsheet and enter the new data. Because of OLE, the chart will take its data directly from the sheet, including your new data, and will update 'automagically'. It looks as though there might be an emerging trend there ... next lesson might be interesting!

USING MS EXCEL IN E-LEARNING

Changing the look of an Excel Spreadsheet

Excel can be used for more than just holding student records, it can be used to create interactive learning materials, however the look of a spread sheet can easily put of even the keenest student. With a little bit of tinkering a spreadsheet can be made more interesting to look at by formatting the cells and inserting images.

Using Colour in Spreadsheets

The spreadsheet can be made to look visually more appealing by formatting the cells and inserting a colour. To do this;

— Highlight the columns and on the format menu, click on format cells.

— Next click on the patterns tab and select a colour

To get rid of any unwanted text which is required by the graph, change the font colour to the same as the background Alternatively, by formatting the sheet, you can insert a background Finally you can add comments by using the inset comment function on the Insert Toolbar.

Producing interactive graphs using slide bars

Sometimes, it is useful to have a simple animation to show students, when teaching a particular principle. This can be important with graphs or sets of data. Many graphs can be altered by the insertion of a variable into the formula. Then, by altering this variable the desired effect can be made. To do this in Excel you can do this using you can use either a slide bar or spinner, as can be seen in the example below.

To insert a spinner or scrollbar you need to obtain another toolbar in Excel. Click first on View dropdown menu, then Toolbars and then Forms. This brings up another toolbar on the screen, which can either be left floating or dragged up onto the toolbars at the top or the page.

On this toolbar click on either the Scrollbar (LHS 6 th row) or Spinner (RHS) and then using the left mouse button draw the item in its required position on the sheet. For these to work they need to be formatted. To do this RIGHT click on the scroll bar and click on Format Control. This brings up a box where you can set a minimum and maximum values as well as the incremental change.

Before closing this box, click on the symbol on the Cell link box and then click on the cell where you want the result to be placed. Press return to return to the dialogue box and click OK Move the scrollbar/spinner and it should now work. Finally use this variable figure in any data set or formula to demonstrate the principle

Producing Multiple Choice Quizzes in Excel

Import an Image into spreadsheet using the "Insert then Picture" command. Add background colour, if required using the "formatting" toolbar. Using the "Forms" toolbar (View then Toolbars then Forms) - add a "Combo Box" by clicking on the button (4 th Row RHS) Repeat the process to add all the

"Combo Boxes". Add arrows using the drawing facility to each of the choices

Go to Sheet 2, and add all the possible answers in column 2 with "please select" as the top answer In Column 1, two rows below, add: Student Choice, Correct Answer, Difference, Response underneath each other.

Using the first "Combo Box", type the correct number in the student choice box counting "Please select" as number 1 and counting down to the correct one. In the "Difference" box type in = the box number "Correct Answer -Student Choice e.g. =C17-C16 In the "Response Box" type in =IF(Student Choice Box =1,"",IF(Difference =0,"Well Done", "Try Again")) Highlight the entire boxes that you have completed and drag them across to the adjacent columns up to the number of Combo Boxes that you have. Highlight the correct answer in each and insert this number in the column into the "Correct Answer" Box Linking the sheets. Highlight Combo Box 1 and using the right mouse click on "Format Control" Select the "Control Tab and click on the right image. Go to Sheet 2 and highlight the entire range of answers. Go back to Sheet 1 and the range will appear in the list.

On Format Control, repeat the procedure with "Cell Link" and link it to the " Student Choice" Box on Sheet 2 Place the cursor in Sheet 1 where you want the feedback to be displayed, press "=", and click on the response box on sheet 2 in the appropriate column, this will be where the feedback will go. Repeat for the other boxes Finally to loose the look of a spread sheet click on Tools menu and then , Options. Uncheck the gridlines, row and column headers, horizontal and vertical scroll bars and sheet tabs. The latter one hides the data from the student and ensures that the student cannot tamper with the sheet.

6

Using MS Power Point for Learning

TOOLBARS OF POWER POINT

The toolbars contain graphically illustrated buttons that you click to perform specific tasks in a program. PowerPoint 97 has four main toolbars, which can help you create your presentations quickly and easily.

Standard Toolbar

The Standard Toolbar is located at the top of the PowerPoint window, below the menu bar. It has buttons for common tasks such as saving, printing, checking spelling, and inserting charts and tables.

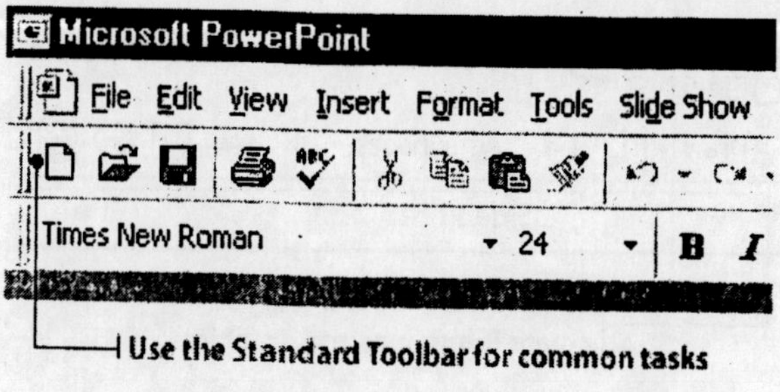

Figure 1. Standard Toolbar of PowerPoint

Formatting Toolbar

The Formatting Toolbar is located just below the standard toolbar. Most of its buttons are for formatting text. Use these buttons to change the font type or size, make text bold or italic, indent text, and insert bullets.

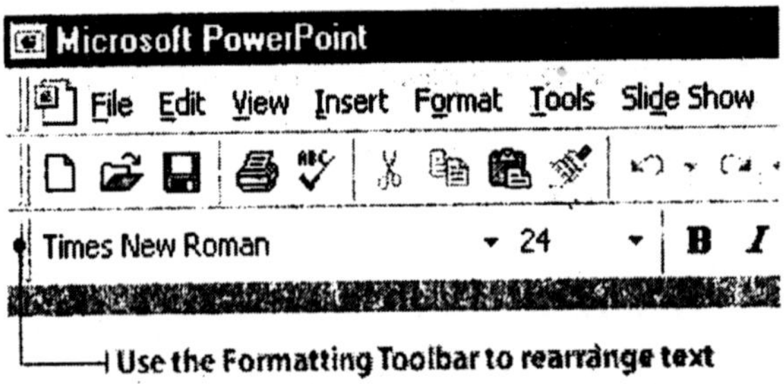

Figure 2. Formatting Toolbar of PowerPoint

Drawing Toolbar

The Drawing Toolbar is located at the bottom of the PowerPoint window. It has tools for drawing shapes, adding lines and curves, and inserting text boxes and WordArt. It also has buttons for manipulating and formatting the objects you draw.

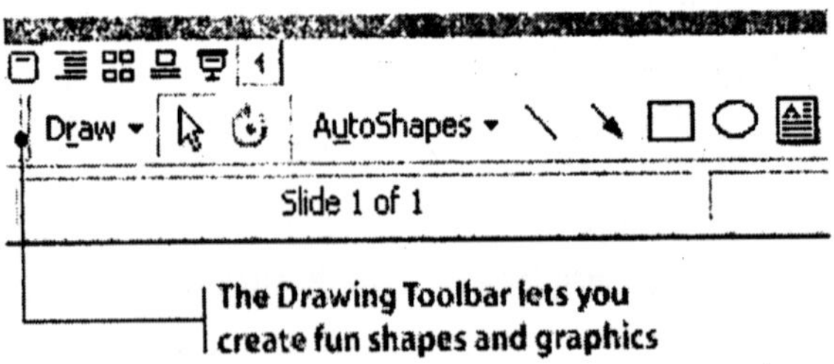

Figure 3. Drawing Toolbar of PowerPoint

Common Tasks toolbar

The Common Tasks toolbar is initially a floating toolbar. That is, it isn't anchored to an edge of the PowerPoint window. Use this toolbar to create a new slide, change the layout of a slide, or apply a design.

Figure 4. Common Tasks toolbar of PowerPoint

If you can't see the Common Tasks Toolbar, you can make it appear using these steps: Click the View menu, point to Toolbars, then click the check box beside Common Tasks. A check mark indicates that a toolbar is activated.

With all these powerful toolbars, things can get pretty tangled up on your desktop. All those buttons must look like the freeway during rush hour.

Moving the toolbars to new locations

All PowerPoint toolbars can be moved or docked to any side of the PowerPoint window. As well, docked toolbars, including the Standard Toolbar, the Formatting Toolbar, and the Drawing Toolbar, can be converted to floating toolbars.

A move handle on the left or top of the toolbar indicates that the toolbar is docked. A title bar indicates that the toolbar is floating.

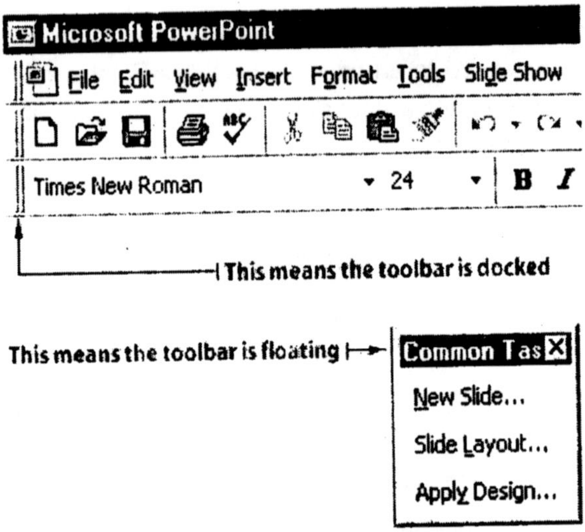

Figure 5. Moving the toolbars to new locations

Here's how to move one of the toolbars to a new location:

1. Click the move handle on a docked toolbar, or click the title bar on a floating toolbar.
2. Holding down the mouse button, drag the toolbar to the new location.

Docking a toolbar

Try docking the Common Tasks toolbar to the top of the PowerPoint window. This will give you more working area on your PowerPoint window.

1. Click the title bar on the Common Tasks toolbar.
2. Drag the toolbar upwards, until the toolbar outline snaps into place along the edge of the program window.

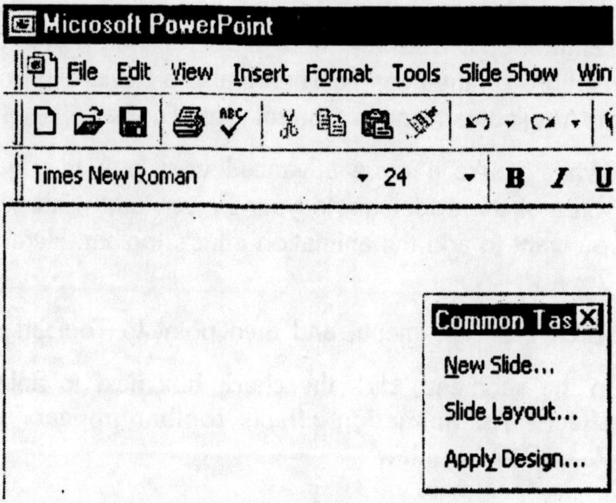

Figure 6. Docking a toolbar

If you see move handles on the toolbar, you know it is successfully docked.

Adding and removing toolbars

PowerPoint has several other toolbars to help you accomplish your tasks.

The Picture Toolbar has several buttons that are useful when you work with images. There are buttons for Contrast, Brightness, and Cropping. This toolbar will automatically appear when you insert clip art or pictures.

The Picture Toolbar appears when you insert an image

Figure 7. Picture Toolbar

The Animation Effects Toolbar has buttons for working with animations, and the Web Toolbar helps you create presentations on the Internet. There's also a Reviewing Toolbar, a WordArt Toolbar, and a Control Box Toolbar.

When you're a more advanced user, you may wish to add some of these toolbars to your PowerPoint window. Let's say you want to add the animation effects toolbar. Here's what you do:

1. Click the View menu, and then point to Toolbars.
2. In the submenu, click the check box next to animation effects. An animation effects toolbar appears in the PowerPoint window.

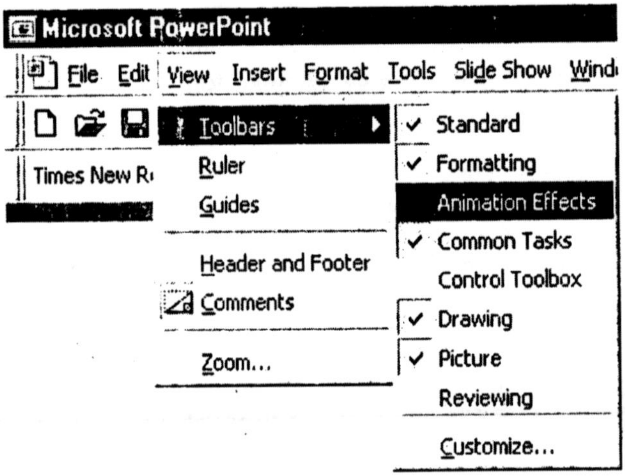

Figure 8. Animation Effects Toolbar

Removing a toolbar

PowerPoint lets you remove toolbars you don't need. Try removing the animation effects toolbar you just activated.

1. Click the View menu, and then point to Toolbar.
2. In the submenu, click the check box next to animation effects to deselect it.

The check mark disappears and the animation effects toolbar is removed from your PowerPoint window

CREATING A SLIDE

Consider you have to create a Title Slide for your presentation using the Blank Presentation option. You will be working in Slide View.

1. Open the PowerPoint program. The PowerPoint dialog box appears.
2. In the PowerPoint dialog box, click the Blank Presentation option button. The New Slide dialog box appears. It asks you to choose an AutoLayout format.
3. Click the Title Slide layout. It's the first in the list. The name Title Slide appears in the preview box.
4. Click OK. A Title Slide appears, ready for you to work with.

The PowerPoint dialog box appears only when you first launch the program. If you are already working in PowerPoint and want to create a new blank presentation, click the New button on the Standard Toolbar or follow these steps:

1. Click the File menu, then Click New.
2. In the New Presentation dialog box, click Blank Presentation, and then click OK.

Adding text to a slide

The Title Slide layout contains text boxes for a title and a subtitle. Try typing text into these boxes.

1. Click in the Title text box. A thick gray border appears around the text box indicating that it is selected.
2. Type a title.
3. Click the Subtitle text box and type a subtitle.

Adding another slide

1. Click the New Slide button on the Common Tasks toolbar.
2. The AutoLayout dialog box will appear. Choose a layout for your next slide.

Okay, so now we have multiple slides for our presentation. But how do we move from slide to slide?

It's as easy as the click of a button. Literally. Just click and you've moved to a new slide.

That's great! You've got the moves.

Moving from slide to slide

Let's say you've created several slides for your presentation. You've finished working on the last slide, and now you want to take a look at your other slides. Here's how you move from slide to slide in Slide View.

To move to a previous slide:

1. Click the upper double-arrow button on the lower right corner of the PowerPoint window. The previous slide will appear.

To move to the next slide:

1. Click the lower double-arrow button on the lower right corner of the PowerPoint window.

OUTLINE VIEW

In Outline View, your presentation appears as an outline, made up of titles and main text from each slide. Because you can see all your presentation in one window, rather than one slide at a time, it's an ideal place to plan, organize, or edit your presentation.

Switching to Outline View

To switch to Outline View, click the Outline View button in the lower left-hand corner of the PowerPoint window.

This is what you should see in Outline View:

When you go to Outline View, PowerPoint automatically displays an Outline Toolbar on the left side of the window. It contains many useful tools for working in this view.

Adding a slide to your outline

You can add a new slide in Outline View the same way that you do in Slide View.

1. On the Common Tasks toolbar, click New Slide.
2. In the New Slide dialog box, click a slide layout, then click OK. A new slide icon appears in your outline.

You can also add new slides quickly by using the Enter key. To add a new slide right after a slide title:

1. Place your cursor at the end of a slide title.
2. Press the Enter key. A new slide icon will appear in your outline.

Adding text to your outline

If you want to add text to a slide that you created previously, click an insertion point in the outline and start typing. If you want to add text to a new slide you've created in Outline View, follow these steps:

1. Type a title beside the slide icon.

2. After the slide title, press the Enter key. PowerPoint adds a new slide.
3. Click the Demote button on the outline toolbar to convert the new slide to a text object.
4. Type your text.
5. To add another bullet point, press Enter.

With the exception of the title slide, any text you add will be formatted as a bullet point.

Moving around in Outline View

When you are in Outline View, you see all the text that appears on your slides. However, PowerPoint lets you collapse the view, so you see only the outline titles. Use this option if you want to print an outline of your presentation, or if you want to check the logical flow of your slide titles without the distraction of extra text.

To collapse all the slides in your outline:

1. On the Outline Toolbar, click the Collapse All button. The slide text for all the slides will disappear.

To expand all of the slide titles again:

1. Click the Expand All button on the Outline toolbar. The text for all the slides will appear again.

Jumping from one slide to the next

To move from one slide to another in Outline View, click anywhere on the slide you want to move to.

AUTOCONTENT WIZARD

The AutoContent Wizard is a good option for creating a presentation if you are a beginner. The AutoContent Wizard offers suggestions for templates to use and types of content to put in. This option is also good if you are in hurry and want to create a presentation quickly.

Creating a Presentation using the AutoContent Wizard.

If you have just launched PowerPoint, click the AutoContent Wizard option button in the PowerPoint dialog box to start a presentation. If you are already working in PowerPoint, here's how you start the AutoContent Wizard:

1. Click the File menu, then click New. The New Presentation dialog box will appear.
2. In the New Presentation dialog box, click the Presentations tab.
3. In the Presentations list, click the AutoContent Wizard, and then click OK. The wizard will start.

Working with the AutoContent Wizard

The AutoContent Wizard will guide you through some simple steps.

1. Read the information on the start screen, then click Next.
2. In the next dialog box, select the type of presentation you want to give, then click Next to advance to the next dialog box.
3. Continue entering options until you reach the Finish step.
4. Click Finish.

The AutoContent Wizard will display your presentation in Outline View. The outline is made up of sample slides, each of which has a suggestion for the type of information that should be entered in the slide. You can customize the information in the slides in either Outline View or Slide View.

TEMPLATES

A template, also called a presentation design, lets you create a presentation without worrying about design elements. The template defines the color, background, and font of the slides. PowerPoint has many templates, which you can preview and select in the New Presentation dialog box. PowerPoint also lets you customize the templates. For instance, you can change the background color or typeface of a template.

Creating a presentation using templates

If you have just launched PowerPoint, click the Template option button in the PowerPoint dialog box to start a new presentation. If you are already working in PowerPoint, follow these steps:

1. Click the File menu, then click New. The New Presentation dialog box appears.
2. Click the Presentation Designs tab, and then click an appropriate template. The design will appear in the preview box.
3. Click OK. The New Presentation dialog box will close.

Saving Your Presentation

While working on a presentation, it's a good idea to save your work often. Otherwise, you risk losing your work. The next steps show you how to save your presentation to your hard drive for the first time, using the Save As command.

1. Click the File menu, and then click Save As. The Save As dialog box will appear.
2. In the File name box, type a name for your presentation.
3. Click Save.

The presentation is now saved to your hard drive. Once you've saved the presentation for the first time, periodically save it by clicking the File menu, then clicking Save. Or, click the Save button on the Standard toolbar.

MAKING CHANGES

Moving a text box

If you don't like where a text box is positioned on a page, you can move it to a new location. First you select it, then you move it.

1. Click the text box you want to move. A thick gray border will appear around the text box.
2. Place the pointer on the border. The pointer will change into a four-headed arrow.
3. Hold down the mouse button and drag the box to the new location.
4. Release the mouse button.

Resizing a text box

The gray border that appears around an object when you select it has square handles on its corners and on its sides. These are called selection or resizing handles. You can click and drag these handles to resize text boxes.

1. Click the text box to select it. A gray border will appear around the text box.
2. Place the pointer on a resizing handle. The pointer will change into a two-headed arrow.
3. Hold down the mouse button and drag the resizing handle until the box is the size you want. Drag outwards to make the box larger. Drag inwards to make the box smaller.

Adding a new text box

Sometimes, you may want to add text to a slide without using a built-in text box. For example, you may want to type a label for a drawing, or you may want to add text to a blank slide layout. In PowerPoint, you can add your own text boxes to any slide using the Text Box tool on the drawing toolbar.

1. On the drawing toolbar, click the Text Box button. The pointer will change to a cross.
2. Click on the slide where you want to place the text. A small text box will appear.
3. Type a word in the text box. As you type, the box will expand to fit the text.
4. After you finish typing, click outside the text box. The border around the box will disappear.

Copying a text box

1. Click the text box to select it.
2. Place the pointer on the box's border and click again. The insertion point will disappear from the text box.
3. Click the Edit menu, then click Copy.
4. Click the Edit menu again, then click Paste. A copy of the text box is now pasted on top of the original box.
5. Click and drag the new text box to the location you want.

Deleting a text box

You can delete your text boxes using the Delete key on your keyboard.

1. Click the text box to select it. A gray border will appear around the text box.
2. Click the box's border. The insertion point will disappear from the text box.
3. Press the Delete key on your keyboard. The text and the border both disappear. The entire text box is deleted.

If you want to delete a built-in text box (one that came with the original slide), you need one additional step.

1. Click the text box to select it.
2. Click the box's border and then click the Delete key. The text disappears, but the border remains.
3. Click the border again and press the Delete key. The entire text box is deleted.

Adding color to a text box

1. Click the text box to select it.
2. On the drawing toolbar, click the arrow beside the Fill Color button, then click the green color box. The text box will turn green.

Outlining a text box

As you have seen, the thick gray border that appears around a text box is temporary and disappears when the text is deselected. If you want a permanent outline around your text box, create one using the drawing toolbar. Try adding a blue dotted outline to a text box.

1. Click the text box to select it. A border will appear around the text box.
2. On the drawing toolbar, click the arrow beside the Line Color button, then click the blue color box.
3. Next, click the Line Style button, and then click 3 pt.
4. Finally, click the Dash Style button, and then click the square dot dash option. A dash style box will appear.
5. Click outside the text box to deselect it.

Changing your font

1. Click the text box to select it.

2. Place the pointer on the box's border, and click again. The insertion point disappears, indicating that the entire text box is selected.
3. Click the Format menu, then click Font. The Font dialog box appears.
4. In the Font style list, click Bold; in the Size list, click 36; and in the Color list, click green.
5. Click OK to close the font dialog box.

All the text in your text box is now green, bolded, and a font size of 36.

Selecting a new bullet style

1. Click anywhere in the bulleted text to select it.
2. Click the Format menu, then click Bullet. The Bullet dialog box will appear.
3. Click the square bullet in the symbol grid.
4. If you want, select a new color for the bullet in the color list box.
5. Click OK. The new bullet style will appear in your bulleted text.

Changing your background color

In PowerPoint it's easy to change the background color of the slide you are working on.

Let's say you want to change the color of the slide to light blue. Here's what to do:

1. Click the Format menu, then click Background. The Background dialog box will appear.
2. In the Background fill section, click the arrow on the list box to open it.

3. Click More colors to open the Colors dialog box.
4. In the Colors section, click a light shade of blue.
5. Click OK to close the Colors dialog box.
6. In the Background dialog box, click the Preview button to see a preview of the slide color.
7. If you like what you see, click the Apply button. The background color of the slide is now light blue.

Changing your background pattern

1. Click the Format menu, then click Background. The Background dialog box appears.
2. Click the Background Fill list box, then click Fill Effects. The Fill Effects dialog box will appear.
3. Click the Pattern tab, and then click the pattern you want in the Pattern box. A preview of the pattern will appear in the Sample box.

Checking your spelling

It's a good idea to check the spelling in your presentation before the audience sees it. Let PowerPoint's spelling checker check the presentation for you. When you activate the spelling checker, it checks the spelling in all of your slides.

1. On the Standard toolbar, click the Spelling button.
2. If a spelling error is detected a Spelling dialog box appears.
3. The Spelling Checker suggests an alternative spelling in the Change To box. An additional list of suggestions may also appear below the box.
4. If you want to continue without changing the spelling, click Ignore.
5. If you want to change the spelling, enter one of the suggested alternatives in the Change To box, then click Change.

After you've made your selection in the spelling dialog box, the spelling checker will continue checking the remaining slides. When it has checked all the slides in your presentation, a message box will appear telling you that the spell check is complete.

Turning the automatic spelling checker off

PowerPoint 97 also has an automatic spelling checker. As you type, a red wavy line appears under misspelled words. If you want to correct the spelling immediately, you right-click your mouse on the word, and a menu appears suggesting spelling alternatives. If you don't want to see wavy red lines under misspelled words as you type, you can turn the automatic spelling checker off.

1. Click the Tools menu, then click Options. The Options dialog box appears.
2. Click the Spelling tab.
3. Under Check spelling as you type, click the Spelling check box to deselect it. The check mark disappears.
4. Click OK to close the Options dialog box. The automatic spelling checker is now deactivated.

The automatic spelling checker is turned off, but the main spelling checker still works. You can check the spelling in your presentation at any time by clicking the Spelling button on the Standard toolbar.

Adding a shape

PowerPoint lets you add a variety of shapes to the slides of your presentation. Try adding a star shape to your slide, using the AutoShape tool on the drawing toolbar.

1. Click the AutoShapes button, point to Stars and Banners, and then click the 5-point star shape. The pointer will change into a cross.

2. Click anywhere on the slide. A star of predefined size will be inserted.
3. To make the shape larger (or smaller), drag a resizing handle. To resize the shape proportionally, hold down the SHIFT key as you drag.

Moving a shape

Let's try moving the star to another part of the slide.

1. Place the pointer on the star. The pointer turns into a four-headed arrow.
2. Click and hold down the mouse button, then drag the star to the new location.
3. When the star is positioned where you want it, release the mouse button.

Adding color and texture to a shape

First, try adding the color yellow to the star.

1. Click the star shape to select it.
2. Click the arrow beside the Fill Color button, and then click More Fill Colors. A Colors dialog box appears.
3. Click the Standard tab, then under Colors, click a shade of yellow.
4. Click OK to close the Colors dialog box.

Next, try adding some texture to the shape.

1. Click the star to select it.
2. Click the arrow beside the Fill Color button, then click Fill Effects. The Fill Effects dialog box appears.
3. Click the Texture tab.
4. Click on a texture, and then click OK.

Adding clip art

You can add clip art to any slide using the Insert Clip Art button on the Standard Toolbar. Try adding a cartoon image to your slide.

1. On the Standard Toolbar, click the Insert Clip Art button.
2. The Microsoft Clip gallery dialog box appears.
3. Click the Clip Art tab.
4. In the Categories list, click Cartoons. PowerPoint displays clip art from the Cartoons category.
5. Click an image to select it.
6. Click the Insert button. The cartoon image is inserted on your slide.

Some AutoLayout slides in PowerPoint already have placeholders for clip art. To insert clip art into one of these slides, simply double-click the placeholder and the clip art gallery will open.

Resizing clip art

Like text boxes and shapes, it's easy to change the size of a clip art image. Here's how:

1. Click the cartoon image to select it.
2. Place the pointer on a resizing handle. The pointer will change into a two-headed arrow.
3. While holding down the mouse button, drag your mouse outwards. This will enlarge the image. If you drag your mouse inwards, you will reduce the size of the image.
4. When the image is the size you want, release the mouse button.

Cropping clip art

When you resize an image, you make the whole image larger or smaller. When you crop an image, you actually remove parts of the image.

The following steps will show you how to crop an image.

1. Click the image to select it. Resizing handles will appear around the image.
2. On the picture toolbar, click the Crop button.
3. Place the pointer in the center of a resizing handle. The pointer will change into a cropping tool.
4. Holding down the mouse button, drag inwards. A part of the image will disappear.
5. When enough of the image has been cropped, release the mouse button.
6. To turn the cropping tool off, click the crop button on the picture toolbar.

Did you accidentally crop off too much of the image? No problem. To restore an image that has been cropped, simply click the Crop button, then click a resizing handle and drag outwards. The cropped portion of the image will reappear.

Adding your own works of art

You are not restricted to using clip art or pictures from the Clip Art gallery. PowerPoint lets you insert images from other sources.

Let's say you've used a graphics program to create an amazing logo for your school, and you want to insert the logo into your PowerPoint presentation. Here's how to do it:

1. Click the Insert menu, point to Picture, and then click From File. The Insert Picture dialog box will appear.
2. In the Look in box, find the drive and folder where the artwork is located.
3. In the File name box, enter the name of the file. Then click the Insert button.
4. The drawing is inserted on the slide.

Layering images

Sometimes you may end up with images overlapping each other on a slide. Let's say you've created a design where three different colored squares are layered on top of each other: a blue square at the back, a yellow square in the middle, and an orange square in front.

You want to send the orange square to the back layer. How do you get it there?

Try these steps:

1. Click the orange square to select it.
2. On the drawing toolbar, click the Draw button. The Draw menu appears.
3. Point to Order, and then click Send to Back.

To bring the orange square back to the front.

1. Click the orange square to select it.
2. Click the Draw menu, point to Order, and then click Bring to Front.

Adding shadows to images

Let's try adding a shadow to a shape using the Shadow button.

1. Click the shape to select it.
2. On the Drawing Toolbar, click the Shadow button, then click a style.

Adding a chart

To add a chart to any slide, click the Insert Chart button on the Standard Toolbar.

When you insert a chart, a sample data sheet and corresponding bar chart will appear on your slide. PowerPoint has included some sample data in the first four columns. The bars in the chart are the graphical representation of the numbers in the data sheet. Notice how a higher number in the data sheet results in a taller corresponding bar.

To create your own chart, you can replace the data in the sample data sheet with your own. Try adding a number to the chart to see how it changes the corresponding bar on the chart.

1. On the data sheet, click in the first row of column A.
2. Type in the number 50, then press Enter. The corresponding bar on the chart increases in height.
3. Try adding other numbers into the data sheet to see how they affect the bars.

Some slide AutoLayouts have placeholders for charts. To insert a chart into one of these layouts, just double-click the chart placeholder.

After you've finished entering data, exit the work window by clicking anywhere outside the chart or the data sheet. The data sheet will disappear. If you need to make any revisions to the chart, double-click the chart and the data sheet will appear again. If the data sheet doesn't appear after you double-click the chart, click the View Data Sheet button on the Standard Toolbar.

Adding and deleting information

The default chart has four sets of bars, and its data sheet has four columns of information filled in. What if your presentation requires more than four columns/bars? It's simple. Fill in additional columns on your data sheet.

1. Go to the next empty column on the data sheet and click inside a cell. Type the numbers 50, 60, and 70 in the first three rows.
2. Notice how a new set of bars appears in the chart.

You can also remove columns or bars from your data sheet and chart. Here's how you do it:

1. Click the column heading of the column you want to delete. For example, Column D.
2. Click the Edit menu, then click Delete. The data disappears from the column and the corresponding bars disappear from the chart.

Changing the type of chart

The default chart in PowerPoint is a bar chart. If you think your information would be better as a different type of chart, you can change the chart type.

The following steps show you how to convert the bar chart to a pie chart:

1. Double-click the chart you want to change. A heavy border appears around the chart, and the data sheet appears.
2. Click the Chart menu, then click Chart Type. A Chart Type dialog box appears.
3. In the Chart Type list, click Pie, and then click OK. The information in your data sheet will now be displayed in a pie chart.

Adding a table

You can add a table to a slide using the Insert Microsoft Word Table button on the Standard Toolbar. Let's try adding a table to your slide.

1. On the Standard Toolbar, click the Insert Microsoft Word Table button.
2. In the drop-down box, click and drag the pointer across the number of rows and columns you want for your table. For example, three rows and three columns.

3. Release the mouse button. The table work window will appear.

The work window is where you enter and edit information, and where you format the table. If you click outside of the work table, the table will disappear. To make the work table reappear, place the pointer on the slide until it changes into a four-headed arrow, then double-click.

The work table is easier to work with if you add gridlines. This way, you can see all the columns and rows. To add gridlines to your table:

1. Click anywhere in the table.
2. Click the Table menu, then click Show Gridlines.

Next, you will type information into the work table.

1. Click inside the first column of the first row.
2. Type the word January.
3. Press the TAB key on your keyboard. The insertion point is now in the second column of the first row.
4. Type the word February.
5. Press the TAB key to move to the next column, and type the word March.

To move to a previous column in a row, press SHIFT + TAB. You can also move around the table by simply clicking where you want to move to, or by using the arrow keys on your keyboard. After you've finished typing, click outside the work table to exit the work window.

Adjusting the height and width of cells

A cell is the box that is formed in a table where a row and a column intersect. Each cell holds a unit of information. In PowerPoint you can adjust the height and width of the cells. The following steps will show you how to adjust the height and width of cells in your table.

1. Double-click the table to enter the table work window. A work table will appear.
2. First, try making the cells in the first column narrower.
   (a) Place the pointer on the gridline between the first and second column. The pointer will change into a two-headed arrow.
   (b) Click and drag the gridline to the left. The cells become narrower.
   (c) Click and drag the gridline to the right to make the cells wider again.
3. Now, make the cells in the first column taller.
   (a) Place the pointer on the gridline between the first and second rows. The pointer will change into a two-headed arrow.
   (b) Click and drag the gridline downwards. The cells become taller.
   (c) Click and drag the gridline upwards to make the cells shorter again.

Switching to Slide Sorter View

When you go to Slide Sorter View, you see miniatures of all the slides in the presentation, complete with text and graphics. This view is useful for rearranging slides, and for adding transitions to slides. There are two ways to switch to Slide Sorter View: Click the Slide Sorter View button in the lower left corner of the PowerPoint window. Or, you can click the View menu, then click Slide Sorter.

Moving slides around

The Slide Sorter View is the easiest place to rearrange the order of your slides. Let's say you have four slides in your presentation, and you decide that Slide 2 should really appear after Slide 3. Here's what you do to move the slides around:

1. Click Slide 2 and hold down the mouse button. A small gray rectangle appears on the pointer.
2. Drag the pointer to the slide's new position after Slide 3. Avertical line should appear after Slide 3.
3. Release the mouse button. Slide 2 should now be positioned after Slide 3.

Jazzing up your table

When you exit the work window, you see the table the way it will look in your presentation. Before you format the table, it looks pretty plain.

Try jazzing up your table using the Table AutoFormat command in the Table menu.

1. Double-click the table you want to format. A work table will appear on your slide.
2. Click the Table menu, then click Table AutoFormat. The Table AutoFormat dialog box appears.
3. In the Formats list, click on a style. A preview of the style will appear in the Preview box.
4. Click OK.

Adding a Transition

A transition is a special effect used to introduce a slide during a slide show.

The following steps will show you how to add a transition to a slide.

1. In Slide Sorter View, click the slide you want to add the transition to.
2. Click the Slide Show menu, then click Slide Transition. A Slide Transition dialog box will appear.

3. In the Effect list box, click Checkerboard Across.
4. Click the Medium option button to select a speed for the transition.
5. Click the Apply button. A slide transition icon appears under the slide's left corner, indicating that the transition has been applied.

If you want the same transition to apply to all the slides in your presentation, click the Apply to All button in the Slide Transition dialog box.

TIMING A TRANSITION

If you want your slide show to run automatically, you must add timing to the slides. When you add timing to a slide, you specify the number of seconds to remain on each slide.

Here's how you add timing to your slides:

1. Select the slide you want to add a timing to by clicking it.
2. In Slide Sorter View, click the Slide Show menu, and then click Slide Transition. The Slide Transition dialog box will appear.
3. Under Advance, click the check box next to Automatically After.
4. In the seconds box, type the number of seconds to remain on the slide. For example, 5 seconds.
5. Click the Apply button.

When you run your slide show, the slide that you have applied the timing to will only remain on screen for five seconds.

ADDING YOUR OWN ARTWORK

When you animate an object, you add special visual or sound effects to it. The following steps will show you how to animate a cartoon image while working in Slide View.

1. Click the Slide View button to go to Slide View.
2. On the slide, click the cartoon image to select it.
3. On the Formatting Toolbar, click the Animation Effects button. The Animation Effects Toolbar will appear.
4. On the Animation Effects Toolbar, click the Flying Effect button. The flying effect is now added to the image.

ANIMATING

Animating Text

Try adding the typewriter effect to text on your slide.

1. In Slide View, select the text you want to animate by clicking it.
2. On the Animation Effects Toolbar, click the Typewriter Text Effect button. The typewriter text effect is now added to the text.

Animating a chart

You can make charts more interesting by animating them. In a Slide Show, an unanimated chart appears onscreen all at once. When you animate a chart, the chart appears "bit by bit". You specify the way the elements of the chart will appear in the Custom Animation dialog box.

Try animating a chart so that the elements of the chart are introduced onscreen by category.

1. In Slide View, click the chart you want to animate.
2. On the Animation Effects Toolbar, click the Custom Animation button. The Custom Animation dialog box will appear.
3. In the Introduce chart elements drop-down list, click by Category.

4. Click OK. The Custom Animation box closes and the animation effect is applied to the chart.

Changing animation order

Normally, the object that is animated first appears first, but you can rearrange the order. Here's what you do:

1. Click the object you want to change. For example, the flying pig.
2. On the Animation Effects Toolbar, click the drop-down list and select the number 1.

Previewing an animation

PowerPoint lets you preview animation settings for your current slide without running the entire slide show.

1. In Slide View, go to the slide you want to preview.
2. Click the Slide Show menu, then click Animation Preview.

A slide miniature appears in the upper right corner. It shows the full animation effects of the slide.

WATCHING THE SLIDE SHOW

In a Slide Show, all the slides of your presentation are displayed in sequence. The Slide Show is controlled either automatically or manually.

You can preview the presentation you are working on at anytime by clicking the Slide Show button. If you have applied timings to all the slides in your show, the Slide Show runs automatically.

If you haven't applied timings to the slides, you must advance the slides manually.

Let's take a look at how you can preview a Slide Show by advancing the slides manually.

1. Click the Slide Show button in the lower left corner of the PowerPoint window. The first slide of the show will appear.

2. To advance to the next slide of the show, click the left mouse button. The next slide will appear onscreen.

3. Continue clicking the left mouse button until the show is complete.

Starting the Slide Show somewhere in the middle

1. In Slide Sorter View, click the slide you want the Slide Show to start with. For example, Slide 5.

2. Click the Slide Show button.

The Slide Show begins with the slide you selected.

Stopping the Slide Show

PowerPoint lets you stop the slide show for any reason. Follow these steps.

1. Move the pointer on the screen and wait for the button to appear in the lower, left- hand corner of the screen.

2. Click the button, and then click End Show. The show stops

ADDING SOUND

Adding sound to animations

Some of the animations in PowerPoint, for example, the Flying Effect, already have sound built into them. But most of the animations do not have sound effects.

In PowerPoint you can add sound to any animation. You can also replace the current sound effect on an animation with a new one.

Try adding a sound effect to an animation.

1. In Slide View, select the animated object you want to add the sound effect to by clicking it.
2. Click the Slide Show menu, then click Custom Animation. You can also click the Custom Animation button on the Animation Effects toolbar.
3. Under Entry animation and sound, select a sound effect from the drop-down list.
4. If you want to preview the sound effect, click the Preview Button.
5. Click OK to add the sound to the animation. The sound is added to the animated object.

Adding sound to transitions

Spice up your transitions by adding sound effects to them. Here's how:

1. In Slide Sorter View, click the slide with the transition you are adding sound to.
2. Click the Slide Show menu, and then click Slide Transition. The Slide Transition dialog box will appear.
3. Select a sound effect from the Sound drop-down list, then click Apply. The sound is added to the transition.

If you want the sound to continue playing until the next sound in your presentation, click the check box next to 'Loop until next sound'. But use this feature sparingly. Some sounds may lose their effect if they are played too long. Or, they may interfere with other elements of your presentation.

7

USING INTERNET FOR RESEARCH

The Internet or the Net is a collection of computers, all link together, to share information globally. It was first developed in the U.S. by two universities who were both working on the same contract and wanted to share their data. They were faxing information back and forth and then retyping it until they came up with a piece of software called *Unix to Unix Copy Program* or *UUCP*.

The Internet was born and has mushroomed outward from that point.

There are 4 things that are necessary to "get on the net" with a full *graphic interface* (picture, sounds, animation, etc...).

— A *computer* - preferably with a fast processor (around 100 MHz or more) and lots of memory (16 meg or more)

— A *modem* - preferably 56,000 baud or high speed digital

— *Browser Software* - often installed with your operating system or can be *downloaded* off the Internet

— An *ISP* - An *Internet Service Provider* is a service that connects your home or office computer to the Internet

Once you have purchased an account with an ISP you will be given an *account name*. This is often your *email address* as well. You will also be given a *password* and should also be provided with instructions on how to change the password to a unique and personalized. The generic password provided with your account should be change to one of your own. Protect your password as you would any personal identification number (PIN) number.

The ISP will also provide information on how to *configure your software*. This can be simple or difficult depending on your *Operating System*. Once configured you simply run the software to connect your computer's modem to the ISP's modem, giving you access to the Internet.

There are a number of pieces of software that work together to connect you to the Internet.

The first and most complicated is the *dialer* or *socket* software. This is the software that makes the physical connection with the ISP's computer and the internet. This needs to be configured only once but you will need instructions from your ISP on how to do this as each ISP has a different setup.

The second piece is an *Internet browser*. This is the program that locates websites for you and allows users to maneuver around (*surf*) the *World Wide Web* and view web pages. The two most popular today are AOL's *Netscape Navigator* and Microsoft's *Internet Explorer* though *Mosaic* was the first and still used by some people.*Opera* is another. Before graphic browsers *Lynx* was the most popular browser and is still available for text browsing. There are also a number of different ones and new ones being developed every once in a while. Some ISP have a *proprietary type of browser* though most have given up this practice as it limits the users abilities to browse the Internet.

Type the url or web address of the website that you want to visit in the *address bar* of your browser and press Enter or click Go. Collect your favorite websites by adding them to your *Favorites* or *Bookmarks*. To go to a Favorite or Bookmark, click on the menu and click on the link.

Another piece of software is an *email program*. This program controls sending, composing and receiving email. Most email programs can also be used to read postings on *newsgroups*.

Instructions for getting this software can be obtained from your ISP though you may have to *download* the newest version yourself.

There are many different ISPs. If you attend a university or college or belong to a military or government organization you can most likely get *Internet access* through your school or work. If not you will most likely buy access from a *commercial provider*.

Another option, if you are in a major center, is the *Freenet*. Many major cities have groups devoted to making the Internet accessible to the greater majority of people and create Freenets which allowing members free access to the Internet. They run on private and public donations. It is an excellent way of learning about the Internet in a helpful environment.

Once you are connected you will have access to *Email*, *Newsgroups*, the *World Wide Web (WWW)*, *File Transfer Protocol (ftp)*, *Internet Relay Chat* (irc), *Search Engines*, *ICQ* and other Internet Services.

EMAIL

Email is the electronic equivalent of sending a letter through the mail. There are many different mail reading programs or applications that control email but the basic functions are all the same. An email address directs a message to the *recipient*.

Email addresses are made up of:

— the *account name* (often the users first initial and then the last name (sometimes only 8 characters)

— then the @ symbol

— then the name of the user's *ISP*

— the last 2 or 3 characters describe the *type of service* called the *top level domain* name. For example *.com* stand for commercial site, *.ca* - noncommercial site in Canada, *.mil* - U.S. military, *.gov* - U.S. government, *.au* - noncommercial site in Australia, *.net* - network, etc... Recently 2 new TLDs were added; .biz, .info.

As well as sending and receiving mail the recipient can;

— *save the address* for future reference in an *address book*

— *reply* to the original message

— *forward* the message to a third party

— *edit* a message

— check the spelling and a wide range of other options.

One of the services provided by your ISP is to provide a storage area or mailbox to collect email in. Email software programs control the transfer of this stored email by *downloading* the messages from your mailbox on your ISP's computer to your own computer. You must be connected to the Internet to do this.

An email message is made up of two parts; the *header* information and the *body*. The recipient's address (to), the subject, the sender's email address as well as other information is contained in the header. The content of the message is in the body. You can find out information about an email message by viewing the header content. Most email programs had a 'view header' option in the menu.

New messages can be written or composed *off-line* (not connected to the Internet). If the ISP charges by the hour, connect to the Internet only to send and receive your email and then disconnect to read and compose your mail.

Some companies offer *free email* service that you can sign up for. These free services rely on advertising for revenue so your recipient will also be receive an advertisment with the email. Usually email is accessed through a web browser where the user composes and reads their mail online. The benefit is that you can easily access your mail from any internet terminal and the address is easily disposable (if it gets added to a junk mail list for instance). The disadvantage is that it doesn't have the legitimacy of a business address and it may be difficult to complete transactions.

You can also *attach* files to email messages to send picture, sound, documents, videos and other types of file with your email. Some email programs automatically open attachments such as photos and html code. Change the program's properties or options to turn this feature on or off.

Unrequested or *spam* email has become a problem on the internet. A large percentage of the email sent is this unrequested email which takes up bandwidth and causes prices to rise. Businesses must take time to sort through spam to find the legitimate email which also takes time and money. Most ISPs provide software that will filter out the worst of this email. If you find that you are receiving a lot of unrequested email contact your ISP to see if they can provide you with *spam filters*.

Email Attachments

An *attachment* is a computer file or files place inside an email message. Email was originally designed to handle only *plain text* (no formatting, ie. bold, centering, etc.) which was transferred from one computer to another in a format called *ASCII*. ASCII is a standard across all computer types which makes e-mail universal. Today many modern email programs allow *HTML* (hypertext markup language) to be included in email messages which allow you to format your email messages with font sizes, bold, centre and such. The recipient must have an HTML capable email reader to see the formatting otherwise they will get a document marked up with HTML tags.

To attach a document to an email message drag the file attachment to the body of the message and drop it. An attachment can also be added by choosing *File Attachment* from the menu. Most modern email programs place a button on the Toolbar usually in the shape of a paper clip that you can click. A dialog box will open that allows you to browse and select the file that you want to attach. You can attach more than one file to a single email message. Don't move the original document until the message has been sent.

Most documents created on computer, such as word processing documents (Word, WordPerfect, etc.) or spreadsheet documents (Excel, Quatro, etc.) or graphic files (Corel Draw, Paint Shop, or .gif and .jpg files) are stored in their own unique *binary code* format. This binary format is determined by the program that the file is created with. Email documents are create as *text files* so in order to send a binary file or document via email, it must first be *encoded* into a text format and then attached to the email text message.

There are several common *encoding standards*, the most popular being uuencoding, mime, and binhex. Not all email packages support even these three, let along all the non-standard ones. If someone sends you a document encoded in a format that your email program doesn't support the email program will not decode the attachment.

The attached file must be loaded into a program to be viewed. If the attached document was originally created in MS-Word you need MS-Word on your computer to work with the document. Most modern *software suites* can *import* documents from other suites, but typically it's best to have the correct matching program.

Most modern email programs work hand-in-hand with your operating system to try and open the correct program required to view the document sent as an attachment. This is done by matching the file extension such as .jpg, .gif, .doc, etc... with a registered *file type*.

Viruses can also be transferred via email attachments. Because your email software handles the decoding of programs sent as attachments it is easy to infect your computer simply by opening an infected attachment. Always check email attachment with an anti-virus program before opening them.

There are several reasons why an attachment will not display properly or at all:

— the encoded file is corrupted and cannot be decoded. This is usually due to damage in transit and happens very seldom these days.

— the encoding type is not supported by your e-mail program and so the file cannot be decoded back to it's original type.

— the attached document was created in a program that you don't have on your computer or is not a registered file type.

— the email program has an option set which automatically locks attached files

When sending an attachment you should think about whether the intended recipient has the same program on their computer. When you are sending an attachment to someone you should always use a standard encoding process (the one that comes with your email program is usally best) and send the document in a format that the recipient can view. If in doubt, ask them first by email.

Macs users should be aware that most Windows user won't be able to decode a binhex file.

If your email software automatically locks attachments and you want to view the attachment you can change the programs settings by modifying the Preferences or Options.

If the formatting isn't important it's better to copy your the text from the original program and then paste it into the body of a plain text email message rather than sending an attachment. Everybody's email software can read this 'plain text' ASCII format.

NEWSGROUPS

Newsgroups are discussion groups that are going on all the time. You can write a message and *post* it to a newsgroup in the morning and come back to read a *reply* to the message in the afternoon. You can also reply to other's messages.

There are thousands of news groups covering as many topics. Some are *moderated*, meaning that a person who has knowledge or an interest in a certain topic will receive the message and read it before posting it. This keeps the discussion on topic. Most are not moderated and the discussion can go anywhere but it can be a great way to get a quick reply to your questions.

One problem with posting a message to a public newsgroup is that unscrupulous companies mine the newsgroups for email addresses and then send *unsolicited email* (*spam*) to the poster. It is recommended that you disguise your email address using your newsgroup software's preferences.

Many newsgroups have a publicly accessible *faq*. A faq is a collection of *frequently asked questions* that have been posted many times to a newsgroup. You may get a gentle reminder or a completely rude and insulting comment if you post a question that is on the faq. It is acceptable to post a question as where the faq is located and you may find that frequent posters will mention the faq in their message.

NAVIGATION

World Wide Web (*WWW*) is a collection of web pages connected together with *hyperlinks*. Each document or page has a unique address that allows you to find it among the millions of other documents on the *Web*. The address is called a *Uniform Resource Locator* (*URL*) or sometimes a *Uniform Resource*

Indicator (*URI*). When you chose a new *link* by clicking on it or by typing it into the *address field* your browser sends a request for that document and displays it on the screen. That link can be to a different section of the current document, another document on the same website as the original or on another website anywhere in the world. Web pages are designed using *hypertext markup language* or *HTML*.

Designing a basic HTML page is not difficult after mastering a few simple codes or if you are planning a website you can have a *Web Developer* create one for you. The key to the web are the links to different, useful or interesting pages. Many web page user will collect links to their favorite *sites* or *web pages* and add them to a *bookmark* or *favorites* list.

Receiving information from another computer is called *downloading*. When a user chooses a web page to go to the browser automatically downloads the information from the page and displays it on the users computer screen. The user can also choose to download specific files. Sending information to another computer is called *uploading*. To place a web page on a website the developer must upload the file from their computer to the ISPs *server*.

Being *Online* means being connected to another computer, whether that computer is your ISP, your friends computer across town or a remote office computer, through a modem, or digital connection. Going *Offline* means disconnecting your computer from the remote connection.

FILE TRANSFER PROTOCOL

File Transfer Protocol (*ftp*) allows users to transfer files and documents from one computer to another. There are a few different software programs that will make this process quite simple. If you are designing a website you can use ftp to update your website. Computer users can also use an ftp program to download files and software off the internet. Many companies and universities offer ftp sites that contain software which can be downloaded and used on your computer. A search for 'ftp' will display dozens of ftp programs that can be used to download software.

Internet Relay Chat (irc) allows users to participate in *real-time discussions* with other users through the Internet. A user logs on to an irc site and then types messages and replies to others messages as they are written. Often an irc discussions has a topic and users will join to discuss this topic. Other irc discussions are free flowing and regardless of how centred the discussion is it can take some time to sort out the different *threads* of discussion in a busy irc. They are also used for online conferences with a famous or knowledgeable person contributing their time to answer questions and present information.

Along the same theme are online *game sites* where Internet users can compete against other users on the Net.

Instant Messaging software, such as ICQ and MSN allows users to find friends and contacts through the Internet and communicate with them in real time. Users maintain a list of contacts which the software will notify when they are online and contact is available. To use an instant messaging service it is necessary to have and register software available on the Internet. Instant messaging allows you to chat, send messages and files and various other features but only with people you choose. Often the software and registration is free.

INTERNET AND RESERACH

If you are looking for a specific company or organization try typing *www.company name.com* into the address bar first. If it is a "country specific" organization try ending with the specific, 2 character country code rather than .com.

Search Engines make finding things on the Internet relatively easier. Search engines are run by companies that collect information from the Internet, sort and categorize it and present the information to the user based on *keyword searches* or through *directory listings*. It is worth taking some time to learn how to make an effective keyword search as the amount of information that these search engines provide can be overwhelming. It is common to be provided with 10s of thousands of references to any given search term. By narrowing your search to a specific phrase you can target your searches more effectively. Many search engines require that you enclose a search phrase in quotes (e.g. "the cat in the hat").

Different search engines will display different results and sort those results differently. If you don't find the information you want on one search site try another. Some search companies offer *meta searches* which are compiled from a number of different search engines' results.

Most search sites offer directory listings as well. The information is categorized in a hierarchy from general categories to specific categories. To find a specific web site follow the links down to the category that matches your interest.

The results from a search are a list of pages with links to the documents that match your search. Each search engine has a different way of displaying the results but generally you will see a list with the name of the organization or title of the page. You may also see a short description of that web page. Clicking on the title will take you to that page.

Though there are hundreds of search engines on the Internet there are only a couple dozen that the majority of people use. If you choose "customize" in your browsers search tool you will see a list of some of these search engines.

Website Search

As well as Internet searches many websites offer a website search feature to help visitors find information on that specific website. Generally there will be a button marked 'Search' beside a text field. Enter your query to display links to the pages that match.

The Internet is a wonderful resource for researchers of all kinds, but like every other kind of research tool there are new skills to be learned and decisions to be made about how and when to use it. This is where your research planning will be important. Some of the points you need to consider are:

— What is your research question? (i.e. what is it you are looking for?).

— What kind of information do you need?

— What *tools* are you going to use to find this information? (i.e. the Internet, the school library)

— How are you going to find this information? (i.e. if you are using *Internet search engines*, what *keywords* are you going to use?)

— How much time are you going to spend researching? (i.e. you could go on forever finding information, but you shouldn't. What would be a reasonable time frame for finding the information you need?)

— How are you going to *evaluate* your information? (i.e. when you are finished your research it is always useful to reflect on the process. What things worked, what things didn't, what would you do next time?).

Looking For Resources

Finding resources on the Internet can be like looking for a needle in a haystack. There are millions of documents on the Internet, published by specialists, scientists, teachers and students. Some of them will be useful for your research project, the trick is in finding them! Luckily there is an array of research tools you can use to locate the information you want.

Directories

One of the easiest and safest methods of researching for relevant resources is by using Directories that have already been vetted by other organisations. Directories are collections of resources organised into categories. Sometimes the directory will focus on one subject area, others may collect and organise resources in a number of areas.

SOFWeb has a number of directories to help teachers and students locate information and resources quickly and easily. The *SOFWeb Resource Centre* has carefully selected WWW resources, subject associations, education officers and other resources which are categorised according to Key Learning Areas and include a brief description about the site.

EdNA is the *Education Network of Australia* which specialises in getting educational resources from around Australia bringing together the best each State and its system has to offer.

Out on the World Wide Web are other directories such as the *WWW Virtual Library* and *Yahoo. Yahooligans* is a sub-directory of Yahoo set up especially for kids. Other useful places to look for subject catalogues of on-line resources are Point Communication Corporation's *Top 5% Sites* which rates and reviews web sites, as does *WebCrawler* which reviews "the best of the net". One of the most useful directories for serious researchers is *The Argus Clearinghouse* which "provides a central access point for value-added topical guides which identify, describe, and evaluate Internet-based information resources." and not forgetting the *Internet Public Library*, the first public library for the Internet community.

Search engines

The internet is not like your school library, with its shelves of well organised books. Simply browsing the internet is unlikely to find you the information you need, so in order to find the resources you want for your research project, you will need, at some point, to use a search engine. Behind the scenes search engines compile databases of web pages which allow users to search the internet for specific resources, by doing what is termed a *keyword search*. When a user types in a search request such as "egypt", the search engine already knows where all the pages including "egypt" are located. The search engines use "bots" or "spiders" which prowl the internet collecting pages, but depending on the search engine, the databases of pages may be more or less up-to-date.

Planning a search

When you are using a search engine it's important to clearly define your keywords. You need to be specific rather than general, because there is so much information out there, a general search may return you hundreds of thousands of hits. In order to avoid being overloaded with information, think carefully about what you are searching for. For example, a search on Alta Vista for the word "cat" returned 500,000 hits! But a search for "cat health" returned only 200 hits, still a large number, but much more useful.

Before you start your search think about what you are looking for and do some preliminary work with a pen and paper. Think of all the possible terms you might use for your subject. Think of any differences there may be in terminology from country to country. For example, in Australia we talk about primary schools, in the US the term is elementary school. So a search for "primary school" might not find you information about American schools. Of course this might be an advantage if you were only looking for information about Australia. For more help with planning your search, see the Learning with the Internet module on Trawling the Net: a Classroom Model

Each search engine uses a slightly different language to help you with your searches, so it is worth the time it takes to read the search guides each engine provides. There are many different search engines.

— *Web Wombat* is an engine which searches only Australian and New Zealand sites. This can be very useful if you are interested in specifically local material and don't want to have to sort through 100s of URLs from all around the world.

— *Alta Vista* is another very useful search engine. particularly as it has an Australian site, which means searches are very fast. Alta Vista's advanced search functions are probably the most full featured on the web, allowing you to create very defined searches.

— *Lycos* is able to search for images and sounds, as well as text files, which makes it very useful if you are looking for multimedia resources.

— *WebCrawler* has a very useful feature, the adjacency search. This means you can specify how close to each other words appear in a document. For example, if you were interested in finding out about Ballarat in the Goldrush era, you might ask to find a document in which the words "goldrush" and "Ballarat" appear within 25 words of each other.

— *Open Text* not only indexes every word of millions of web pages, it allows you to search news headlines from on-line newspapers, including *The Sydney Morning Herald*.

Ask The Experts

One of the best things about the net is the access it gives you to experts in just about any field you might be interested in. From aeronautics to xylophones, you can be sure that someone out there knows all about it and even better, is willing to share their knowledge with you. There are lots of places to go to find experts. You might join an *e-mail discussion list*, participate in a *newsgroup* or access experts through the Internet from PITSCO's *Ask an Expert* site. From here you will find a list of over 300 web sites and e-mail addresses of experts to answer your questions. Before you start asking make sure you check the questions that have already been asked, in case your query has already been answered. In order to make sure that the experts remain willing to share their knowledge with the Internet community, there are some things you can do to make their lives easier and ensure that they remain willing to help.

— Don't ask an expert any question you could have found out for yourself. The experts are a resource for the difficult stuff, not an excuse for not doing the work.

— When you do ask the experts make sure that you have a real question. Asking an aeronautical engineer from NASA what she knows about aeroplanes is a waste of her time. Chances are instead of some interesting information you won't get a reply at all. On the other hand, if you have done your research and ask her a specific question you have not been able to find out about elsewhere, chances are that you will get a useful and informative reply.

— If you are doing research in a group or as a class, try to ensure that you don't flood the experts with a dozen of the same question. If you are going to post a question, decide as a group what it is going to be, and then nominate one person to ask it. You are much more likely to get a reply this way.

— If you have posted your question to a newsgroup or e-mail list chances are you will get several replies. It is polite and interesting if you offer to compile the answers you receive and post them back to the list, so everyone can share in the information.

— Be patient if you don't get an immediate answer. Most people have one or two other things to do and answering your question may not be high on their list of priorities, strange as it may seem.

— Say thank you. That way next time you, or someone else has a question the on-line experts will be happy to answer.

EVALUATING RESOURCES

Finding the information you want on the Internet is only the first step. There is a lot of material available, but not all of it is equally reliable and useful. As a researcher a large part of your job is not simply to find information, but to make judgements about its merit. Before you use any material you have found, you need to spend some time evaluating it for accuracy and importance. Use the following questions as a guide, but also use your own experience and skills to make a decision.

Evaluating Internet resources is not that different from evaluating other kinds of resources, many of the questions about such things as authority, bias, and currency will be of equal importance. The source of the material might give you a clue to it's reliability. A site maintained by a university or government organisation might be more reliable than one maintained by a private citizen.

Sometimes the age of information matters. If you need current statistics then check the age of the material you have found. As a rule of thumb, in most fields anything more than five years old is probably out-dated. But a site which deals with historical information may not need up-dating as frequently as one which is all about the latest political events. Just because information isn't regularly changed doesn't mean you shouldn't use it, but you need to be aware that your information is not necessarily the most recent.

The status of the writer is often of considerable importance in deciding the reliability of information. You can probably assume that material written or otherwise provided by a known expert in the field is likely to be reliable. Resources provided under the auspices of a recognised institution might be considered reliable as well. But what about student pages on a university server? Just because you have never heard of the author of the page doesn't mean that the information is inaccurate or unreliable, but it does mean that you can't take it at face value. You might have to do some cross-checking, either elsewhere on the net, or with books or articles.

Who put the material on the Internet and why? Think about whether they might have some reason other than pure helpfulness for posting information. Many special interest groups have web pages, and while this doesn't necessarily meant the material is biased it is something you need to think about. All sorts of groups now have web pages on the Internet, and obviously all of them have a message they are trying to get across. Think about what is being said, and why the material is there.

Think about ways you might cross check the information you have found. You might have a look at another site with similar material, ask somebody who knows something about the topic, have a look at book on the subject. Use your own experience as well. If you have already done some research in the area you will already have some knowledge of the subject. How does this material fit in with what you already know? How an Internet resource is designed may have a lot of influence on how you use it. A site which is always too busy to access, too slow to download or too difficult to navigate may not be worth your valuable time, no matter how useful and relevant the information is.

PLAGIARISM & REFERENCING ELECTRONIC RESOURCES

Referencing (also called citing) simply means that you indicate which material is not your own and show where you got it from. Even if you have not used someone's exact words, but have rephrased their ideas you need to give your sources. The idea is that someone else reading your work should be able to recognise the difference between your work and someone else's. You need to provide them with enough information about your sources that they could find the source for themselves. There are several different referencing systems, each subject area tends to use it's own system of citations, but whatever style you choose it is important to be consistent, complete and accurate. This is matters not only for books and articles, but electronic sources as well.

Plagiarism is theft. If someone broke into your house and stole your television you would be understandably upset. That was your television and now you can't watch *The Simpsons*. In exactly the same way, using someone else's ideas without acknowledging where they came from is stealing.

That is what referencing is all about, making sure that you if you use someone else's words or ideas, you let your readers know where the information came from. It is okay to quote from a book, or use the ideas from someone's work in your own work, but it does mean that you need to be careful to make sure that you acknowledge where the information came from, and make it quite clear that it is not your own original ideas. The way you do that is to make sure you reference any material you use which is not your own.

8

Using Internet Communication Tools in Classroom

The nearly universal availability of Internet access to students has prompted many instructors to incorporate online tools as supporting elements of their regular courses. An instructor using online tools as a significant support component for a class or course will often create an "online learning system" that includes two or more of the tools commonly used in online instruction. Often, these tools are individual software applications, such as an email sending and reading application, or a Web browser for reading World Wide Web pages.

To support the instructor seeking to design an online learning system, this chapter describes the most important tools to consider, and provides criteria for evaluating their applicability to a particular teacher's needs. Although it is primarily intended for instructors with limited expertise in the field of online educational tools, it provides all instructors with a set of criteria for evaluating and selecting components for an online learning system that is most appropriate for their needs. This chapter does not provide detailed reviews of individual software examples, nor does it instruct in how to set up online learning software. It is intended as an overview of the types of tools and technologies that are currently available to teachers who wish to incorporate online tools as part of their class materials.

Note that online support for most courses will not need every tool described below, and that each course must be evaluated individually to determine which functions provided by these tools would be useful. Integrated systems, combining two or more of the commonly used tools, must be evaluated in terms of their support for these essential functions. The tools listed here are described specifically with regard to their use for education. They are presented in terms of their,

1) specific characteristics,
2) general ease of use for accessing and extending course resources,
3) synchronous or asynchronous character, and
4) advantages and disadvantages for particular purposes.

Various terms are used this chapter with specific meanings. An "online learning system" is the set of tools an instructor selects to provide online support for a course. A single "tool" within an online learning system is an independent software application, or part of an integrated system, that provides one of the primary functions from the list set out below. Any online learning system will include one or more of these tools. The "course resources" are the subject materials that can be read or otherwise accessed online by students, which may be created entirely by the instructor or initiated by the instructor and then supplemented by students. An "individual resource" is a single file, page, or message that is created and used as a unit.

Nearly all online educational tools may be described as one of the following types, each of which is described in greater detail later in this chapter. The most commonly used tools in an online learning system are:

— Archived Messaging Systems

— Static World Wide Web Pages

— Text-Based Conferencing

— Online File Repositories

— Voice-only and Video Conferencing Systems

— Whiteboards

— Special Application Workspaces

ARCHIVED MESSAGING SYSTEMS

This category includes a variety of tools that have existed since the earliest networked computer systems, and is the most widely used asynchronous discussion mechanism. They are "asynchronous" tools because class participants do not all need to be using the tool simultaneously for effective communication. Examples of tools in this class are newsgroups, bulletin boards, and email lists with archiving. These all provide the ability to create and retrieve text-based messages, and a long-term archiving system that retains these messages for future review.

Systems that don't allow archiving are generally not as useful for teaching, and therefore only email lists with associated archiving are included in this group. These tools may all be described as asynchronous, primarily text-based, archived, shared messaging systems. Although they may differ in their precise structure and the tools used to access or maintain them, archived email lists, newsgroups, and bulletin boards all serve essentially the same function for education.

The critical function a messaging system provides is to facilitate public question-and-answer sessions, as well as providing a forum for asynchronous discussions.

Archived messaging tools have the advantages and disadvantages of all asynchronous discussion tools, in that participation does not require attending the forum at specific times, that development of discussions tends to be slow, and content may tend toward considered exposition instead of "inspirational" thinking. Some form of archived messaging tool is probably essential for any online learning system.

The important characteristics of archived messaging systems are:

— It is easy for both the instructor and student to access and extend the course resources.

— They provide an archived set of question-and-answer or discussion resources that grows throughout the course.

— Individual resources are "messages" that are linked to related messages by "threads" that share a common "subject" label, and which are further organized into "mail lists" or "forums" each covering some general topic. This mechanism typically provides only linear or a branched tree organization of indicivdual resources.

— They may include the ability to associate graphics and other media with the message, either by integrating them within the message body, as attachments that can be saved as independent files, or both.

— Resources are typically both created and accessed through the same software application.

— Access to individual resources may sometimes be available through a Web browser, either because the archiving system makes message available through Web pages, or the Web browser contains integrated email and/or newsreader tools.

STATIC WORLD WIDE WEB PAGES

This category includes the majority of Web-based resources, which are "static" because they remain essentially unchanged once they are published (dynamic Web pages are described below in association with integrated learning environments). Web pages may be considered a sophisticated version of the traditional paper "handout," with support for multimedia information embedded within a page, and non-linear organization provided by hyperlinks between pages. Although Web browsers can be used to access materials of many types and not just Web pages, static Web pages are the most common individual resources provided by instructures using the Web as a tool.

The critical function of static World Wide Web pages is to provide a stable "fact repository" resource for participants to use either once or many times during a course.

The important characteristics of static Web pages are:

— It is easy for students to access the individual resources, but creating resources can require special skills.

— Course resources in this category are usually created and extended only by the instructor, since doing so requires some training.

— They are exemplary at integrating text, graphics, and other multimedia information all within a structured page.

— Individual resources are described as "pages" that are linked to related pages by "hyperlinks," and that are organized by "Web site." This mechanism allows nearly complete flexibility in structure.

— Design and structure issues, within single pages and Web sites, must be addressed by the creator to build a coherent resource that promotes understanding and easy use.

— Resources are accessed using a "Web browser," but are typically created and posted online through a variety of different software applications that are independent from the Web browser.

TEXT-BASED CONFERENCING

Text-based conferencing is a synchronous (real-time) communication medium that allows conversational discussion online. It is sometimes called "text-chat," and provides a mechanism for several people to converse through lines of text each created by a participant and displayed to all other participants sharing the same "room" or "forum."

Text-based conferencing is almost never a good environment for "lecture" style teaching, since it is slower than voice communication and when used passively it engages the attention less effectively than a corresponding face-to-face situation. Lecture-type material is better presented using one of the asynchronous teaching tools, then supplemented with text-based conferencing for live discussion.

Although large groups may be supported if suitable moderator and floor control functions are provided, text-based conferencing is generally more engaging and effective for learning when used with small groups (fewer then 25 participants) in open discussion. Large group question-and-answer sessions are better supported by asynchronous messaging systems, which obviate the need for all participants to be using the resource simultaneously.

The critical function a text-based conferencing system provides is a live discussion forum within which questions, answers, and ideas may be rapidly proposed and developed. This promotes "stream-of-consciousness" and "inspirational" thinking.

Note that some text-based conferencing software is now graphically based, sometimes even including "characters" that are graphical representations of the user and from which the "speech" is emitted. These are almost invariably somewhat gimicky systems intended for social chatting, and the graphical aspects typically provide no advantages over plain text systems for educational uses. Such systems may, however, provide particularly easy to use interfaces in some cases.

An unusual feature of text-based communication, as opposed to some other synchronous communication media, is "multi-threaded conversations." These are sessions where more than one topic is discussed simultaneously, with lines of text for each interspersed. Participants skilled in recognizing when a line of communication is referring to one topic or another most often use multi-threaded discussions actively.

Although specialized support for multi-threaded conversations may be available within a given tool, the fact that experienced participants will often leap into multi-threaded conversations, disregarding such support, suggests such suppoprt is only useful for participants new to this mode of communication.

Although multi-threaded conversation is an extremely effective mechanism for increasing the density of communication, which is particularly useful if there is significant lag between when someone enters and line and others receive it, it does require some skill and experience to use effectively. Some students may find multi-threaded live conversation very confusing, and effective moderation by the instructor can amelorate this.

The important characteristics of text-based conferencing are:

— The instructor and students can easily participate equally.

— Communication by text-based conferencing may be slower than voice, although multi-threaded conversation can increase the information flow significantly.

— Participation in discussions is through specific client software, which usually connects to a central server that receives and distributes communications as they are submitted.

— The client software through which the discussion forum is reached usually provides logging facilities for individual participants to record a transcript.

— Access to chat rooms through a Web browser may be possible if the central server, Web browser, and any associated accessory software supports this.

— Logging features may be provided by the server in better systems, whereby transcripts of the sessions may be easily made available to the entire class or to the public.

— Effective participation in discussions may require participants to have good typing skills.

ONLINE FILE REPOSITORIES

Certain courses, in which sharing resources created by students is critical, benefit from the availability of some form of online file repository. In this discussion, an "online file repository" is specifically one for which students may at their own discretion both post and retrieve individual resources in the form of files. Courses incorporating static Web pages may sometimes use their Web site as an online file repository, since the Web system supports hyperlinks pointing to individual resources other than Web pages. Often, but not always, the same software used to post Web pages for creating static Web sites may also be used to post files other than Web pages to online file repositories. The critical function an online file repository provides is the ability of students to easily share with an entire class the file-based resources they have created.

In most courses an online file repository is not needed, and it is sufficient or even desirable to have students submit file-based individual resources to the instructor, who then makes them available through a Web server system. Omission of an online file repository may also be preferred in the case when course resources will be publicly accessible, or when the instructor otherwise wishes to screen what becomes part of the total course resources. However, if sharing student-created files is critical, and doing so only through the instructor would be a burden, an online file repository is a useful tool.

The important characteristics of an online file repository are:

— Both the instructor and students are able to access and extend the course resources.

— File-based individual resources may typically be of any type, including, for example, movies, word processor documents, or spreadsheets.

— Separate software applications are usually used to post files and to retrieve them, with Web browsers commonly used for the latter function.

VOICE-ONLY AND VIDEO CONFERENCING SYSTEMS

Voice-only and video conferencing systems, with the latter invariably incorporating voice also, are synchronous communication mechanisms that transmit live sound and images to all class participants. The primary features of voice-only and video conferencing systems are that they do not require skilled typing to achieve nearly face-to-face rates of communication, and, depending on their quality, they may support vocal inflection and facial expressions as additional communication channels. Both one-to-many and many-to-many systems exist, although only many-to-many systems (allowing full student participation) are considered here.

As with text-based conferencing, material presented as lectures (one-to-many) is typically presented more efficiently using an asynchronous method such as Web pages. Live one-to-many conferencing systems have no advantages over pre-recorded voice or video, which may be made available within static Web pages using "streaming" technology that obviates waiting for the complete resource to download before starting.

A critical weakness of voice-only a videoconferencing systems is that the software supporting them will typically not run on all platforms likely to be used by students. Standards are only now being developed in this area, but instructors should be cautious about requiring their students to use a system that doesn't provide both Mac and PC versions of the software.

Voice-only and video conferencing systems provide a learning environment that closely resembles the traditional classroom. This can be a particular advantage in the case of instructors or students who are dismayed at the prospect of being required to use new tools for teaching and learning.

Although facilities for full-screen real-time video conferencing are available using dedicated links (both land-line and satellite based), these are typically expensive, and often require that special equipment be available at all sites where instructors and students are physically located. For this reason, only Internet-based voice-only and video conferencing systems are considered here, although they usually provides at best choppy video with images smaller than the full screen display. At this time, most people do not have video cameras on the computers they use (either at home or in the workplace), eliminating video conferencing as a generally viable tool for teaching when equal student participation is required. However, inexpensive cameras are rapidly becoming available and this may change in the near future. Until that time, voice conferencing may be more commonly used.

Aside from the hardware required for voice-only conferencing, which is inexpensive and easily obtained, voice processing software must be of good quality and be run on sufficiently fast computers. Although the quality of voice conferencing software applications has recently improved dramatically, most do not support more than one-to-one conversations. In addition, most people do not have sufficiently fast computers or modems to run the software (typically at least a 120 MHz computer and 28 Kbaud or faster network links are the minimum required for barely effective use). Finally, in cases where student participation is involved, floor control when there are no visible facial cues can be complex, although some systems support various mechanisms to remedy this.

Although voice and video conferencing using the Internet may become effective online classroom tools in the near future, this is unlikely to happen until more instructors and students have access to faster computers, and technologies faster than traditional modems are widely used. Video conferencing will certainly not be widespread without the general use of much faster network links than modems. Although Internet-based voice and video conferencing tools are worth watching, it may not be until the end of the decade before they become generally effective online educational tools.

The critical function voice-only and video conferencing systems provide is the ability to communicate at nearly the speed of face-to-face discussions, incorporating vocal inflection and sometimes facial expressions, without requiring the participants to have typing skills.

The important characteristics of voice-only and video conferencing systems system are:

— They provide synchronous communication, promoting rapid development of discussions and "inspirational" thinking.

— They depend upon all participants have access to advanced software, hardware, and network support.

— They provide for the inclusion of vocal inflections and facial expressions as supporting mechanisms for communication, which can greatly aid in understanding.

— They obviate the need for good typing skills in discussion participants.

WHITEBOARDS

Whiteboards are essentially online sketchpads or chalkboards, which may be used either in a one-to-many or many-to-many format. Whiteboards may be used to display a preexisting image that is then annotated, edited, or shown with an active pointer, or may simply provide a blank page on which material is drawn. They are a synchronous communication medium, in which drawings and images are the primary material conveyed.

In most cases, the use of whiteboard for presenting new material is not as effective as making that material available through an asynchronous medium. However, whiteboards are very effective for enhancing discussions in which material is being developed by dynamically editing jointly viewed resources. Materials such as graphical representations or mathematical equations may be presented well using whiteboards. Certainly texts that are jointly created by a class during discussion can also be effectively developed and presented using a whiteboard. Although few independent whiteboard tools are available, they are an increasingly common component of integrated learning environments.

The critical functions a whiteboard provides are a shared display for graphical or drawn resources, and a mechanism for quickly displaying jointly and dynamically developed material.

The important characteristics of whiteboards are:

— They are a graphical synchronous communication medium, almost always used in conjunction with a synchronous conversational medium such as text-based, voice-only, or video conferencing.

— They provide a sketchpad for sharing and dynamically modifying graphical resources, or for displaying jointly and dynamically developed material.

— Because of the need for a parallel conversational channel, they are almost always found incorporated into an integrated learning environment, and only rarely exist as independent applications.

SPECIAL APPLICATION WORKSPACES

Special application workspaces are software tools that provide a simulation or other workspace that is useful for presenting a specific and limited subject area. Some examples are a software application that presents a medical anatomy lesson, one that presents a graph corresponding to a user-specified mathematical equation, or one that simulates a combustion engine and allows its operating parameters to be manipulated.

Since these tools are invariably applicable only to limited subject areas, they are only worth considering if there are examples applicable to the particular course an instructor is designing. Unfortunately, very few special application workspaces have been designed for use online. Even fewer allow several participants to simultaneously use the same individual resource, which is a particularly effective mode for use in conjunction with text-based, voice, or video conferencing. Most special application workspace software has not been developed in a fashion allowing it to be run on any type of computer, so instructors should be cautious abour requiring their students to use such resources. However, the proliferation of Java as a platform-independent programming language for small online applications may lead to the development of many more special application workspaces, which can be integrated into Web pages to supplement other course resources.

The critical function of a special application workspace is the provision of a simulation or workspace that teaches a very specific subject, and therefore may be better able to do so than most general purpose tools.

The important characteristics of special application workspaces are:

— They are only used to teach a specific subject.

— They are at this time only rarely available for online use, or as a shared synchronous tool.

INTEGRATED LEARNING ENVIRONMENTS

Integrated learning environments combine two or more of the tools described earlier in this chapter. The simplest have only two components, usually either archived email and static Web pages, or text-based conferencing with static Web pages. Integrated learning environments provide a common interface that can be simpler than that provided by using a set of independent tools. The consistent interface can speed the process of learning to use the system, and be less likely to intimidate instructors and students with the ordeal of learning to use a new software application each time a new tool is incorporated into the course. In addition, integrated learning environments are typically developed specifically for education or training, and may include features such as support for online examinations and monitoring of which individual resources each student has accessed.

Integrated learning environments sometimes use dynamic Web pages, incorporating Web page forms as the interface to a dynamic database. For instance, a dynamic Web page may display real-time data from a dynamically developing system such as traffic flow. Such systems may generate all their Web pages dynamically, based upon information in the underlying database, rather than simply serving a set of static texts that were prepared earlier. Dynamic Web pages with forms can provide an interface for modifying both the integrated learning system itself and other dynamic databases that may be accessed through the integrated system.

One special class of integrated learning environment is the online virtual world. These systems simulate a physical space, with rooms that may be navigated and objects that may be manipulated. Individual resources presented by such a system appear as objects with functions and behaviors specific to the type of object.

For instance, notes may be read, and bulletin boards may have messages posted on them. Virtual world systems may include a 3D interface (the popular conception of "virtual reality"), but those used for education are primarily built around a Web interface, allowing text, graphics, or multimedia information to be associated with objects found within the virtual space. Non-graphical virtual worlds have been used in formal education for several years, demonstrating that virtual world systems may be used effectively by instructors and students. One particular strength of educational virtual world environments is that they are sometimes extendable by students, who can use the system's simulation facilities to construct "reports" built out of virtual world components that reflect their knowledge and understanding of the subject material.

At this time, very few integrated learning environments are available. Also, the available software does not consistently achieve the primary advantages of an integrated learning environment: more uniform presentation and simpler controls. However, almost all effective contemporary integrated learning environments may be accessed with any up-to-date graphical Web browser, so instructors and students are usually quick to achieve a basic understanding of how such systems function. Support for non-graphical Web browsers is inconsistent, which is a serious consideration for classes that may include non-sighted participants.

The critical function an integrated learning environment provides is a unified interface incorporating two or more Internet-based tools commonly used for education.

The important characteristics of integrated learning environments are:

— Two or more Internet-based teaching tools are incorporated within the single software application.

— Instructors and students access all functions within the system using a consistent interface.

— They may require that only a single, monolithic server software application be set up by technical support staff, instead of many independent tools.

INTERNET TECHNOLOGIES IN CLASSROOM : PLANNING AND IMPLEMENTATION

Use the Internet for reinforcement of concepts already learned in the classroom. It is so exciting for teachers to see students enthusiastic when they find information that we've talked about in class.

Use the Internet for practical application of theoretical principles. Encourage students to apply what they have learned using the Internet as a tool to find examples to make concepts more easily understood.

How Much Time Will It Take to Integrate Internet Into the Curriculum? Just like any planning, it takes time. The more time you spend preparing before class the better the students will respond. The most time consuming part of integrating the Internet is finding sites that work for the unit you are doing. Just about any topic will have a few web sites you can use. Start with a unit that you love, and surf to find sites that have educational value. The key is to visit them before your students do!

Never take a class and set them loose on the Internet. This is just asking for trouble!Students need direction and purpose when using the Internet for educational purposes or they will "surf" to a page about Dennis Rodman instead of Edgar Allen Poe.

The very first time you take a class into the Internet Lab, it is best to have the Computer Technician or another teacher helping you out. Spend at least 20 minutes orienting everyone to the browser that is set up on the computers. All students should be required to listen and go through the presentation, no matter if they are already familiar with the system. The more the students know about how it works, the less problems you'll have down the road.

The best way to keep students on task in the lab is to have tangible goals. They need to know what their purpose is.

After Have Chosen a Topic, How do teacher Go About Organizing the Lab? The best results occur when students have a piece of paper in hand. This gives them purpose, direction, and limits where they go. Always do your homework as a teacher! Use several search engines to find a handful of great sites that students can go to in order to get the understanding that you want.

To make a handout, include the following:

1. Prelab questions: Make sure these are not objective questions, but ones that take higher-level thinking skills.

2. Have at least three to four addresses that you know contain the information you want them to find. That way they have no excuse for not knowing where to look!

3. Have precise directions of how to do a "Net Search." Explain what search engine you want them to use (Yahoo, Web Crawler etc.). Give them the keywords with which they can narrow their topics and/or subcategory links they should select.

4. The handout should consist of questions that are reasonable, and that they will find on the webpages that you have suggested. Be sure these are questions that are above and beyond the textbook or notes the students already have. These questions should be above and beyond what they know.

5. Have some objective questions, like definitions, or ask for "at least 3 details about ___ that we did not talk about in class."

A wide variety of tools is available to the instructor designing Internet-based support for a course, which can be especially complicated for those new to this subject. Fortunately, these almost all fall into a limited set of categories, and the instructor must simply decide which of the categories are appropriate for the particular course, and then either choose one tool from each of the desired categories or select an integrated learning environment that includes such tools.

As a minimum, Internet-based course support typically includes archived email lists for asynchronous discussion, static Web pages for "handouts," and, increasingly, a text-based conferencing system for real-time discourse either as "office hours" or as a live forum for discussing course material. Courses in which students meet in-person only a few times, or not at all, can especially benefit from a synchronous communication component. At this time, instructors choosing just a single online tool for supporting their course have little need for the additional complexity of an integrated learning environment. However, those using two or more tools should at least consider integrated systems, since they can significantly decrease the time required for both instructor and students to become proficient with the tools newly incorporated into the course.

Nearly all the online learning tools described here require some support from expert services. Such support usually consists of setting up the initial software for central servers, and then providing assistance to the instructor in learning to use the tools. The existance of consistant institutional support for such expert technical services is probably critical for expanding the use of online tools beyond a few pioneer teachers. Outside support organizations may also be helpful. The strong advantages of an effectively integrated learning environment when several tools will be used suggests that they will become the most popular systems in the future for courses in which online support is a major component. However, the relatively new appearance of these tools means they are generally harder to use than they could be, limited in features, and sometimes expensive.

9

Legal and Copyright Issues Regarding Downloading Material from the Internet

The widespread availability of access to the internet to a wider world public has effectively made all would-be web authors into 'publishers' on an international stage. Nowadays, publication has devolved to anyone who owns a modem link between the domestic telephone line and a desktop computer. Internet connection is already available through a variety of other means - digital television and internet enabled WAP mobile telephones to name but two - without the need of a computer at all. These global communications exist without geographical barriers, are largely unregulated and take no regard of different time zones. Literally, anybody can publish to the internet, without reference to any body of authority or any required permissions - this is its great strength, but it may also be an inherent weakness.

As it stands now, the internet is not only a broad and invaluable source of freely available information but it also contains much material that is trivial, offensive and of the poorest quality. So much material, in fact, that it is virtually impossible to control or regulate. Laws concerning fraud, libel, etc, exist, of course, but little has been enacted to specifically control and regulate the content of material on the internet thus far, and control, such as it exists at all, has been largely left to individuals to apply within their own limited spheres of influence.

Therefore there is a pressing need to consider what forms of regulation do exist and of the ways in which they affect web authors and the institutions or employers for whom they work. Where once paper-based printing companies had to formulate guidelines and regulations for themselves and had only local and national laws to consider, there are now European and world jurisdictions to take into account.

Since the days of Gutenberg and Caxton, print shops have possessed what came to be known as "Printer's Bibles" - manual of procedures and regulation for use within the print shop. In the United Kingdom, a degree of uniformity and consistency was created and maintained by the Universities of Oxford, Cambridge and London, though it was the late 19th century before even these august bodies could agree on simple spellings of common English words. Nowadays we have to take account of the existence of American, Australian and other lesser known versions of the English language.

Although no definitive manuals exist for internet applications, new legislation is being enacted even as these guidelines are being written. Many other apparently unrelated laws exist which apply equally to the internet, including Race Relations and Sexual Discrimination Acts, Official Secrets Act and the Criminal Justice and Public Order Act of 1994. Other organisations, like WC3 and the BOBBY organisation attempt to bring order into chaos and offer solutions to an otherwise unregulated medium.

LAWS REGARDING DOWNLOADING MATERIAL FROM THE INTERNET

The copyright law and the courts have provided exceptions to the rules which govern the behavior of teachers, students and schools. In general terms, teachers are allowed to make "fair use" of materials for instructional purposes. "Fair use" has been interpreted to include those limited uses which are not likely to deprive a publisher or an author from income. A teacher might make a copy of an article or a page from a book for use with a class to support a particular concept, but they may not make copies of the whole book or workbook for the entire class and use the copies as class texts. They are expected to buy them. For a detailed description of which practices have been shown to be permissible under the law, check the Bellingham Board Policy on Copyright which was drafted by an attorney with copyright expertise.

Some people who work in schools wrongly and illegally take an overly broad view of "fair use" arguing that almost any taking and use of printed materials, software, videos or graphics is permitted because education is a good cause. The law simply forbids such behavior and provides for heavy fines against organizations and employees in caes of violation. Excessive photo-copying has been ruled illegal as has inappropriate use of "home rental" videos is schools and pre schools.

When applied to the Internet and the World Wide Web, the concept of "fair use" and copyright is distorted by longstanding rebellious (and illegal) attitudes expressed by Internet pioneers who have described the Net as a place where text and graphics belong to all "takers" without strings or restrictions.

Aside from ethical considerations, the risks attached to ignoring these laws grow with the size of your mortgage and the resources of your institution. A legal suit is more likely launched against major institutions where the lawyers can establish a case which will influence millions. An individual Internet pioneer could afford bravery and flirt with piracy. A teacher has no business doing so.

"Fair use" of Internet resources by teachers should probably parallel use of print resources. Teachers might make limited use of some text and graphics within their own classrooms.

They probably should not "publish" those same materials across other classrooms within the building by posting on a local area network (LAN) or across other classrooms in other buildings on a wide area network (WAN) or the World Wide Web.

In general terms, students might make rather liberal use of information, text and graphics so long as their resulting works remain within the classroom setting. The moment the works move out of the classroom, they may fall under a "public performance" clause of the copyright law which imposes much greater restrictions and fees. We must distinguish between "practice" publishing and "real" publishing.

Music teachers are usually aware that their students may sing various works within class without extra fees, but if they wish to hold a public performance and charge admission, they will probably be charged royalties. The type of audience and the type of publishing or performing are key factors in assessing appropriate action.

As a general rule, neither teachers nor students may safely make use of other's materials (graphics, text, etc.) when they publish on the Web unless they have requested and received formal permission to do so.

CONCEPT OF INTELLECTUAL PROPERTY

As we work with students and colleagues to identify appropriate copyright behavior, we might focus some attention on the whole concept of "intellectual property" and how it may affect their own futures. All too often we hear Internet radicals calling for free information, declaring that the words and art of all should be community property - free for the taking. This is an insidious notion. It has about as much ethical and logical merit as the arguments of those who defend shoplifting by attacking the large corporations who own the stores.

Some day students' own futures as writers, artists and photographers may be shaped by the laws and court decisions on intellectual property. If these mental products became community property, they would find it even harder to make a living as an artist or writer.

There is also an argument to be made about quality. If you are looking for excellent professional information on cancer to help you and your spouse make a decision about a confusing list of treatment options, you probably do not want to rely upon the casual research of someone with no credentials, experience or research background. You will look for someone with expertise. The development of such expertise and professionalism usually requires years of advanced study as well as many months of research into particular topics. If someone devotes hundreds of hours to learning about an important topic, they deserve a return on their investment.

If we do not respect the notion of "intellectual property," we will sacrifice the incentives which help motivate the writers and artists to make great contributions to the society. Students can learn how their own behaviors either support or undermine a healthy and productive intellectual and artistic community.

As we saunter down the city street, we come across a young woman serenading the passersby with sweet and gentle music. We pause and lean against a utility pole, savoring the deeply moving gifts. Her voice is deep and full of emotion. We recall our own mother's lullabyes the warm ending of childhood days. A half an hour slips by before we realize. Her guitar case lies open before us, a few bills and coins lying there suggestively.

Many schools have purchased clip art collections to use with their students. How this art may be used is defined by the licensing agreement which accompanied the product upon arrival. In most cases, the agreement is printed on some kind of seal which is broken upon opening. In order to determine whether or not you are permitted to publish these images on your Web site, you must see how they describe publishing in general. In most cases there will not be specific language outlining your Web rights. You must employ parallel reasoning.

Most of these agreements require you to print a credit line on any document which you are publishing which includes one or more graphic from the collection. This same approach will probably meet the terms of most licensing agreements, but you cannot take anything for granted. The best advice is to read the agreement.

Unless there is a clear statement that art, photos and text are "public domain" and available for free use, the best policy is to assume that they are copyrighted and should not be taken and used for re-publication on a local area network, a wide area network or a Web site.

Internet pirates argue that work is not copyrighted unless there is a clear notice on the Web page or site. This simply is not the case. Copyright law protects work even if no papers have been filed with the government.

Most people agree that students may use these items for school reports, but some companies are extremely aggressive about their icons and logos. They do not take kindly to abusive use of their company images. Caution is advised. If permission is granted, the best policy is to provide a credit line near the item or at the bottom of the page.

Student work is intellectual property and deserves protection against piracy as much as adult work. Many school districts have taken to posting copyright notices on the bottom of all such pages.

Most schools are careful not to publish the full name of students for safety reasons. In those cases where a potential publisher wishes to contact a student and a family for permission to publish work, it is best to forward the request to the family and let them contact the publisher if interested. For example, in Bellingham, student work may not be published on a Web site unless both the student and the family have signed a release form. Copyright still belongs to the child and the family. If the students are 18 or older, of course, they may sign their own releases.

WEBWHACKER FILES

WebWhacker is a software product which "captures" Web pages and allows you to save them to the hard drive of your computer or to a district file server. In some districts, they are utilizing WebWhacker to create "intranets" which allow students and staff to enjoy Web experiences without ever leaving the district network. There are some great advantages to collecting Web pages locally. This strategy results in much faster access than real Internet access and it allows districts to focus student exploration on pages and sites which meet district curriculum standards and goals.

The danger of this strategy is the copyright issue. Before downloading any pages from a site, the district should obtain explicit, written permission. Despite what some of the software companies may tell you, those pages probably belong to the owner of the Web site and wholesale copying and republication on a WAN is probably illegal.

In many schools, the first home page and Web site emerges as the project of a computer club - perhaps a half dozen students and a faculty advisor. In all too many cases, the group proceeds without much knowledge of school law and without much awareness of the risks. They may have the best intentions in the world. In all too many cases, the Web site develops to a large extent without administrative oversight. This is dangerous. Someone in authority should designate a staff member in each school to keep an eye on the Web site and the legal issues which may arise when a school engages in global publishing.

THE CONCEPT OF COMMUNITY VALUES

Slander

Publishers must always be on the watch for slanderous materials. In the case of schools, the courts have held that libel, slander and damaging reports in high school newspapers are grounds for damages. The school is expected to protect individuals from such damage by reviewing content. Given the reality that Web publishing may reach a global audience, the damages resulting from malicious publishing may far exceed those formerly associated with school newspapers which might have reached several thousand readers.

The courts have ruled that schools have the right to limit freedom of expression in publications in cases where that expression might conflict with community values. While most would argue the importance of allowing students a good deal of freedom, providing a vehicle for individuals to broadcast their beliefs may be another matter.

Freedom of Expression vs. Censorship

Censorship is abhorrent to many of us. In the past, schools published the writings of very few students. The urge to censor was rarely indulged. Editors and a natural emphasis upon quality kept the flow to a trickle. The Web, on the other hand, opens up a whole new approach to publishing which is vastly larger in its implications. We may be in the ironic position of increasing the censoring temptation if we are not somewhat cautious about that publishing.

10

Computer-Mediated Communication in Distance Learning

Throughout the history of human communication, advances in technology have powered paradigmatic shifts in education. Technology changes both what we can do and what we decide is best to do; big shifts in culture cannot occur until the tools are available. The printing press is an example. Before its invention there were people who could read and write; yet not much reading and writing took place because, for one thing, books were costly and scarce. The press enabled widespread literacy, with books accessible and more affordable for all. The spread of literacy in turn changed both the educational system and the class structure, with consequences that still shape our attitudes today.

When people began to accumulate knowledge through the technology of writing and reading, they found a way to preserve it through succeeding generations without relying on memory — greatly changing the way education was conducted. The impact of the printing press on students of the time has been analyzed and reanalyzed. No longer did students have to write or remember everything the teacher delivered; students could use books. But they did not completely give up the oral/aural connection; witness the popularity of lecture classes even now.

As new technology enables shifts at the level of delivery, old technologies are augmented, not totally replaced. Even though many of us have computers at our disposal, we still use books, speech, and pen or pencil writing in education.

More recently, the general availability of electricity has fostered an almost universal use of such inventions as radio, television, and, increasingly, computers. For decades, educational technologists have likened the impact of television and other electronic ways of presenting information to the impact of the printing press on learning. Although to date television has not had nearly the impact on school learning that books have had, we have yet to determine whether its impact on education as a whole will be as great and long lasting. Schooling is only a part of education.

Much of education takes place outside of schooling, both as planned activities and unplanned learning. We may not understand the instructional goals of the Music Television (MTV) channel broadcasts, and those goals may differ from those of educators, but that does not mean MTV viewers do not learn anything. Ultimately we must consider what kind of world we as educators want to build. If we envision the merger of computers and telecommunications as a new tool for teaching and learning, now is the time to clearly articulate and promulgate our goals in order to shape future uses of instructional technology.

EDUCATIONAL SYSTEMS

For communications to take place, at a bare minimum, there must be a sender, a receiver, and a message. If this message is intended as instruction, then besides student, teacher, and content, we must also consider the environment in which this educational communication occurs — an environment that benefits the educational system in some ways and constrains it in others. Part of this learning environment can include various technologies and media. If "the medium is the message," that is, if technology changes what we can do and how we think about it, then the various media enabled by instructional technology also change both what we can do in education and how we conceive of it.

For many years, educators have been exploring ways to combine theories of differing learning styles and student-constructed knowledge with the theory of practice-centered learning. Instead of being passive recipients of knowledge, we now consider students capable of constructing their own knowledge with guidance from the teacher. We can offer part of this tutorial guidance by setting up an environment that will provide students with the resources necessary for independent exploration. In using emerging computer-based technology as a resource, students are encouraged to explore their own interests and to become active educational workers, with opportunities to solve some authentic problems.

As an agent for socialization and collaboration, the networked computer has an even greater potential in education than does the stand-alone, knowledge- server type of computer. The active environment of social learning provided by a computer with access to local, national, and international networks increases interaction and communication among students, their teachers, peers, parents, and other members of the world community. Although there are some differences between distance education and classroom education, the significant issues concerning the use of computer networking and other emerging technologies to promote learning in both are similar.

FROM DISTANCE EDUCATION TO DISTANCE LEARNING

In addition to being entertained, viewers seem to learn from the Music Television (MTV) channel's eclectic mix of music videos, news, instruction, and information on the world of popular music and performers. Broadcast at a distance, MTV's educational content appears largely unplanned in the sense that educators are not directly involved. However, the distance education now originating from universities and colleges attempts to plan educational content and activities for students removed in place and time from their instructors.

Historically, we have not done a very good job of implementing the concept of learner-centered education in distance education. As Thornburg points out, it is difficult, at best, to instill a mindset of lifelong learning in others if we do not understand it and demonstrate it ourselves. One of the reasons that we have failed in this area has been that the tools were not available to do much besides deliver education (as opposed to enable learning) at a distance. Now, computers and telecommunications have opened the way to formats other than pen- and-paper correspondence courses and allow for a more interactive, integrated learning environment.

The type of change enabled by computer-mediated communication (CMC) does not just involve adding new technology to old ways of organizing teaching and learning (Moore, 1993). Although the perennial problem is still one of instructional content and design, we must not pave over old cow paths. In the following chapters, we discuss how education is changing. The paradigm shift is from a teaching environment to a learning environment.

Another notion current in educational circles is that we need to develop motivated, skillful, lifelong learners. As knowledge in many fields increases exponentially, we cannot hope to fill up students as if they were passive, empty vessels. During formal schooling, aspiring professionals can only begin to take in the amount of information that they will need during their career life times. The knowledge base of certain fields may have appeared static for decades, but we can no longer accept that view. Therefore, we must teach students to become lifelong learners by helping them locate the resources to continue learning.

Distance educators are now beginning to focus on a related set of notions:

(a) there are different learning styles,

(b) students create their own meaning when learning new things, and

(c) what makes a difference in content retention and transfer is not so much what is done by teachers, but what students as learners can be encouraged to do themselves.

Much has been written about the importance of accommodating the learning styles of different kinds of students. Suffice it to say here that too often students have little choice in what to learn, how to learn it, or when to learn it. The body of literature on constructivism which has emerged over the past few decades has also contributed to our understanding of learning styles. When content is meaningless to the students' world view, when they are taught as if they were passive recipients of knowledge, or when they have little engagement in the instructional tasks, students have no incentive to construct their own knowledge and little motivation to retain information or transfer its use to novel situations.

The notion of practice-centered learning (PCL) is also important to distance learning. As we learn more about how learning occurs, it becomes increasingly clear that the educational process takes place in a complex internal and external environment. One of the teacher's roles is to become the creator of an effective external learning environment that stimulates the environment within. How do teachers and developers of instruction create environments that are conducive to and enhance student learning?

The technology that can help provide these new environments for education is emerging. This technology allows us to utilize such methods as cooperative learning, to recognize such concepts as interdisciplinary needs in education, and to provide an environment in which collaborative efforts are rewarded. These methods foster a view of knowledge in which expertise is distributed and created among the different participants. Now there is no shortage of technology, only a shortage of the educational vision necessary to use the technology to create new educational environments.

11

Evaluation of Internet-based Information and Student Projects

EVALUATING INTERNET-BASED INFORMATION

Today, when a high school junior is asked to write a report about the Holocaust, a topic that his/her class has not yet discussed. At home the student uses his/her computer with access to the Internet to research the topic and word processing software to construct the report. He/she spends an hour searching the Internet and examining a variety of web pages about the subject and selects some web sites that are particularly compelling because of the graphics and layout of the pages, indicating authority.

The students copies text from the pages, carefully paraphrases some, quotes others, downloads images and pastes them into the appropriate spots on her file, prints a professional looking report, and proudly turns it into the teacher two days later. They used the Internet to explore, discover and report information about this historic event and her word processing software to craft a rather impressive looking information product.

As can easily happen today, each of the web sites that our student used were published by neo-nazi and white-supremacist organizations portraying a biased point of view —

and our youngster's report becomes a reflection of this divisive perspective without the student even knowing it.

This kind of scenario has many educators concerned about using of the Internet as a reliable resource for academic information. The fact is that almost anyone can now publish on the Internet, while only a few years ago, nearly everything that you read was filtered by editors and presented based at least on its economic value if not for its scholarly worth. Today, anyone with an axe to grind can do so over the Internet and with a look of authority. At the same time the Internet is increasingly becoming the first and preferred source of information for many of us.

The presence of inaccurate and biased information on the Internet is not our primary problem. The information and points of view have not really changed, it is the tools that have changed. Today, our students use professional and sophisticated information tools and global electronic networks to complete their assignments while most of us used pencil and paper and the information resources that existed in our school library. While we did our work with what could be compared to a $12 box of Lincoln Logs, students today have at their disposal professional tools and virtually limitless materials, as if they have an entire Builder's Supply warehouse to work from. While we assembled our reports with children's building blocks, today's students can craft their information products with word processors, enrich them with multimedia mined from the Internet, and empower them with hypertext. Their work can be compelling and it can be published to a global community.

The real problem with the scenario above is the assignment. The problem is that we are still, by and large, giving Lincoln Log assignments — "Write a report about the Holocaust." These advanced and powerful capabilities that are increasingly available to our students beg for a different kind of assignment. Writing a report about something has as its goal the demonstration of gained knowledge. Yet gaining knowledge becomes only a small part of what students should be learning to prepare them for a world where knowledge changes and information grows at dizzying speeds. In fact, in the information world, their jobs will be to help in growing knowledge by becoming information builders.

From the perspective of the builder, our students have aisles of information processing tools to choose from and an Internet warehouse from which to choose building materials. The difference is that the builder, in the middle of Builder's Supply, has a task or project in mind, something that he or she plans to build for the enjoyment and convenience of thers. Our builder has a goal behind his or her selections of tools, lumber, and nails.

Likewise, as students browse through the Internet, looking for information raw materials, they to should have goals for their work. Students should be building their information products to affect impressions, decisions, beliefs, support or defeat positions, or create new knowledge.

Goals-based projects have a variety of benefits:

— Goals-based projects provide a context for the student's work that is authentic. They are collecting, synthesizing, processing, assembling and expressing information for a reason that is real and beyond the pursuit of just a grade.

— Students are less likely to simply copy and paste large chunks of text as they would if they were writing about something. They will find and copy smaller chunks of information and then carefully assemble them to produce information products that are designed to accomplish something. They will also provide mortar between these building blocks to hold them together and lend them relevance to the expressed goal.

— Goals-based assignments also lend themselves especially well to the use of rubrics. The student's goals can become part of the rubric's goals, with teacher or student defined benchmarks.

Goals-Based Evaluation

What do goals-based assignments have to do with evaluating Internet resources? Let's return to the builder's analogy. When you are building something in the workshop, the number one key to success is using the appropriate tools and materials. Walk into any "Builder's Supply," and you have a virtual Internet of tools and building materials available to you. As you examine them individually, they are not judged as good or bad, but simply appropriate or inappropriate for specific building projects. The task is to select the tools and materials that are appropriate to our goals.

Traditionally, Internet resources have been evaluated from the perspective of the information itself and it's source. This usually involves some type of checklist that puts all Internet information through the same sieve, evaluating each based on the same criteria.

As students' information products should be based on teacher or student established goals, evaluating the material that they consider using in their products should also be goals-oriented. Rather than judging the material based solely on itself via an examination instrument that has nothing to do with the students work, it should be judged from the perspective of what the student wants to accomplish.

Under certain circumstances, a web page published by a neo-nazi organization might actually be appropriate for an assignment, while other resources, produced by people with credential would not. It depends on what the student wants to accomplish.

This approach actually serves three interesting purposes.

- The student is focused on drawing supporting or appropriate information into the project rather than just filtering "bad" information out.
- The student gathers information about the information.

— As students approaches information with their goals to accomplish, they are less likely to be influenced by the goals of those who generated and published the information, which has interesting implications for media literacy.

Information about the Information

The second benefit is of particular interest as Internet-based information meets with increasing suspicion. In the print-based world, it is only necessary to mention the author's name and a vague reference to the source. "John Robinson said in his book, Acres of Sound, that...". This plus a standard citation placed at the bottom of the page or in the bibliography alone is sufficient to render the information fact.

This will not be enough justification for information gathered from the wild Internet. Other rationale will be needed which might read like this:

John Robinson, in his twelve month research at the University of Hawaii on the influences of motor sounds on the navigation of sea mammals , states that...

This more elaborate explanation of the information's source lends it credibility when a mere URL would not. Therefore, part of the evaluation process should be to identify and collect this sort of supporting information about the information, as justification.

EVALUATION OF INTERNET BASED STUDENT PROJECTS

One of the greatest benefits of using the Internet in the classroom is to provide educational opportunities for students based on their abilities and interests. For example, teachers can teach a basic lesson on a writing strategy and allow a student who is interested in and motivated by baseball to find examples of the writing strategy on a baseball-focused Web site. This lesson suddenly becomes more motivating, exciting, and memorable to this student. Brain research shows that individuals remember events and facts in more detail for a longer period of time if there are emotions involved in the initial learning experience. This concept of emotional memory is highly useful as we use the Internet in our classrooms. Due to the timeliness and currency of the Internet and the fact that students can find information that naturally interests them, the Internet can increase the emotional impact of lessons, and making learning interesting, fun, and meaningful to students.

This section discusses the use of individual and class projects using the Internet to help students experience the joy of learning for themselves. As students gain experience learning for the pure joy of learning, their emotional interest, intrinsic motivation, and hunger for knowledge also increase.

Types of Projects

There is no one right way to use projects in your class. Some teachers prefer to schedule time in the weekly schedule for students to work on projects. Some teachers have students do the majority of project work as homework or as extra credit work. Still others like to use a mixture of classroom time and homework time.

Projects can be divided into several different categories, all of which can be used to enrich the curriculum, strengthen Internet skills, and provide integrated and thematic learning opportunities. Each type of project can be structured as individual student projects, in-class collaborative learning groups, or class-to-class interactions. Don't feel that you must use all of these types of projects. Classroom time is precious and you may want to only use one or two types of projects all year.

Information Literacy Projects

These projects relate directly to the skills discussed in Welcoming the Internet Into the Classroom. Students can choose a subject they would like to learn more about and progress through the six skills. They should be asked to submit proof of all stages in the information literacy spectrum beginning with identifying the big picture task and ending with a product.

Curriculum-Focused Projects

These projects are based on the curriculum content areas and are designed to enrich and teach students about a specific subject. Students should be provided with a list of Web sites that can help them complete their project. Remember to have students write down the Web sites they use to complete their project.

Theme-Focused Projects

These projects are based on the theme being used in the curriculum and/or classroom. These can be supplemented with visits to specific Web sites that relate to the theme. For example, you may have an endangered animal theme in which you could ask students to choose an endangered animal to study and make a presentation about.

Individual Projects

The use of projects has been one of the most motivating teaching techniques, while simultaneously being one of the easiest and most efficient. When students work on individual projects, they can strengthen research and organization skills while being responsible and self-motivated — all skills they will need in the Information Age.

The use of short- and long-term projects provides individual learning opportunities for students tailored for their growth and academic achievement. Projects provide students with choices, meaningful context, and valuable learning time to make sense of the information they are learning. As students work on their individual projects, teachers have time to provide immediate feedback on an individual basis, reducing the fear of failure which many students naturally bring into the classroom.

Teachers can provide students with a calendar and teach them how to use the due date as a starting point and then plan backwards. Arough draft should always be completed three to five days before the due date to give time for last minute changes and editing.

Teachers can teach students the different editing symbols and have them practice editing their own work.Project time is a very quiet time in the classroom and we discuss that movement and talking need to be at a minimum.

The different resources of information available to students: Teachers will take a few days to discuss different information resources available for students. They can discuss the Internet and tie in the discussion with information literacy skills. One of these days includes a trip to the library to review how to look up books, the different resource books available, and how to ask the librarian for help.

Last, teachers can talk to students about their final presentation. They can discuss neatness, spelling, and punctuation, making their project visually appealing, and having a professional look.

In-Class Collaborative Projects

It seems that book after book discussing future workplace skills focuses on the abilities to work effectively with others and to manage information. By teaching students information literacy skills and allowing them to work on projects, students are able to strengthen their skills of managing information. Yet how do we teach kids to work effectively with others? One technique is to integrate projects with in-class collaborative groups. These collaborative teams are designed using heterogeneous student groupings, with each team member having specific roles and responsibilities designed around Internet research and projects.

In-Class Collaboration Steps to Success

Lesson Goals and Objectives: Identify what you want students to learn and be able to do through their collaborative project. This includes identifying the end product and clearly articulating this to students.

Internet Resources: Select Web sites that enhance the project, or develop collaborative learning opportunities based on available Internet projects. Scholastic's Internet Field Trips are a great resource for finding teacher-approved web sites that are grouped by subject.

Team Identities: Create teams using heterogeneous groupings of students. Change groups on a regular basis so that students have the opportunity to work with a wide range of individuals. Have each team choose a name to foster a team identity.

The Big Picture: Make sure teams understand their eventual goal and the time line for completion. Help team members identify their individual roles and responsibilities in order to reach their team goal. It is also helpful to have teams write down the different tasks that need to be addressed and in what order.

Working Time: Give teams time to work together, both on and off the Internet. Some groups will need constant supervision, while others will enjoy the independence of working together.

Timely Reminders: Provide time updates so students aren't caught off guard by an impending due date.

Celebration of Learning: Have teams share their end product and what they learned in a presentation to the entire class.

Reflection Time: Let teams "debrief" by discussing first as a team and then sharing their results with you or the class. Have teams reflect on their group interactions and how effectively they worked together. Let students write down what they observed as the team worked together. Did everyone do his or her job? Did everyone contribute? The power of this type of reflection is that it brings group work into a more conscious light when team members realize they might be receiving indirect feedback from their teammates.

Class-to-Class Projects

The Internet also provides wonderful opportunities for you to work with other classrooms and individuals throughout the world on a common project. These types of collaborative projects come in many different sizes and colors. Remember to start small; join one to two projects a year and see how it goes. As you search for the right project, keep your curriculum and learning objectives in mind.

Collaborative Project Types

Electronic Correspondence: Keypals. This type of project is the equivalent of pen pals and is one of the most common types of projects used in classrooms. These correspondences can be done on a student-to- student basis or as an entire group. Visit the eMail Classroom Exchange site if you are interested in participating in or just want to learn about keypal projects.

Data Collection and Analysis: Some projects ask participants to participate in the collection and analysis of data. This can be as simple as completing a survey, or you may be asked to report weather data to a central site location each week. Check out "Vote Now!" in Scholastic's News Zone for an example.

Information Exchanges: Classes contribute to compilations of information, research, games, jokes, tales, and other things.

Student Publications: Students can publish their original work in an online newspaper, poetry anthology, or magazine. Visit Stone Soup for an example of a student publication.

Virtual Adventures: Online field trips bring students into experiences they would never otherwise participate in or learn about. Through the Internet, students can experience the Iditarod or work in the field with a scientist at Wild Animal Watch: Wolves. In many cases, students can exchange ideas or ask questions of the experts as part of the project experience.

While some of these projects require a sponsoring organization to set them up, others can take place between individual classes or among a small group of interested schools.

Implementing Collaborative Projects

Keep it simple: Start with an easy electronic mail project in which students or your class can exchange small amounts of information.

Once you join, stay involved: Since these projects are collaborative, it is important that you and your class stay committed to the completion of the project. Follow through on your promise to submit information or data.

Be flexible: You will always experience new challenges every time you use the Internet due to its constant evolving changes. Be flexible and keep an open mind.

Ask for help: Don't be afraid to ask for help if you are experiencing difficulties using the Internet or are confused about what is expected of you once you begin a project. Contact the project administrator or get a more experienced teacher or parent volunteer to help

12

Using Computers in Educational Planning and Administration

Teaching in a school or college requires a number of tasks to be undertaken outside the classroom. Some of these are directly related to what goes on in the classroom, such as preparing lessons and marking students' work. Other tasks are of a more general nature. Regardless of how these tasks have come to be required, many of them can be significantly eased by the sensible use of computers. The purpose of this chapter is to suggest ways in which computers can be used to lessen the administrative burden of teachers. Obviously, computers cannot help with every task that teachers are asked to do, and so this site does not contain a comprehensive list of tasks. The suggestions are intended to give you some ideas about how to tackle certain tasks. In order to avoid having large chunks of text, the advice is mostly in the form of bulleted or numbered lists. The suggestions are allocated to tasks. These requirements sometimes arise naturally from the job itself, are sometimes decided by the school or college authorities, and may or may not have a basis in Government policy.

COMPUTER IN EDUCATIONAL ADMINISTRATION

It is generally accepted as good practice for a school or college to have an IT policy for the curriculum, covering such things as access to the computers, how they are used and maintenance. There should also be a similar policy for the administration system, since there are several aspects of its use that can affect everyone.

What should be included?

— Security, including physical security, virus protection, keeping the data secure and access rights

— Data protection

— Copyright laws

— Replacing of equipment

— Staff training.

ALLOCATING STAFF TO TEACHING GROUPS

There are really two problems here:

— To make sure that the numbers work out correctly

— To make sure that the right teachers are allocated to the right groups, which is a matter for the Head of Department's judgement and expertise.

There are several ways in which you can solve the staff allocation problem:

— *Use pencil and paper*: If the department is very small, you will almost certainly find it quicker not to fiddle about on a computer.

— *Use a spreadsheet*: This can be a very useful tool even if only used in a very basic way. For example, you know how many lessons there should be each week for each group, and how many lessons there are in the timetable, including non-contact times. By using the spreadsheet's SUM function appropriately, you can easily spot when the numbers don't add up correctly.

If you have a very large department, you can make greater use of the spreadsheet's hidden powers, and automate the process still further.

— *Use a timetabling program*: For most departments this would be overkill. However, if you manage, say, 20 learning support assistants, some of whom are part-time, and all of whom are allocated to individual pupils rather than subjects, a dedicated timetabling program may be the best option.

You can use either a stand-alone program, or the timetabling module of your admin software suite.

ASSESSMENT & RECORDING

Should you buy a program (or module of a larger program) for assessment and the recording of that assessment, or should you develop in-house solutions? Here are the relative advantages and disadvantages of each.

Commercial programs

Advantages

— Most of the work has been done for you

— They usually let you enter data in batches, via an optical mark reader (OMR)

— If you use an admin suite of programs, the assessment and recording module can be linked to others, like the reporting module.

Disadvantages

— They are usually designed for use by the whole school or college rather than individual subjects

— They go out of date when the rules change, so make sure that provision is made for this in the price

— They may not always be flexible enough to handle a range of assessment and recording requirements.

In-house solutions

Advantages

— They are tailor-made for your requirements

Disadvantages

— They may not be as feature-filled as commercial programs

— They are time-consuming to set up and maintain

General considerations

Whichever approach you adopt, you will need to set up certain procedures. For example,you may want to set up a system whereby marks are transferred from teachers' markbooks to the assessment program via an OMR. If so, you need to think about the staff training required.

In many respects the management of assessment and recording is more difficult than the technical aspects involved.

MAINTAINING CALCULATED RECORDS

If you are maintaining calculated records of any kind, you should take into account the following factors:

— *Different kinds of data*: For example, if the program you use can recognise dates as a data type, format dates as dates, and not as text. This will enable you to do calculations based on dates, if necessary (such as how many days have elapsed since a pupil last handed in homework).

— *Correct date formatting*: Where the program you are using can only treat dates as text, write dates down in the format Year-Month-Day.

— *How numbers are sorted*: In order to ensure that numbers are sorted correctly, place a zero in front of single digits.

CALCULATING STUDENT ACHIEVEMENT

The term "student achievement" can be used to refer to examination or test results, value-added calculations, the number of merits or commendations awarded, and so on.

The DIY solution

A good spreadsheet, such as Excel or 1-2-3, can handle text as well as numbers. You can set up a spreadsheet to record information such as whether a student handed an assignment in, how many times they have not handed in their assignment, the mark they were given for the work and the resultant grade.

Points to consider

Plan the spreadsheet on paper

Assume that you will want extra functionality once you have started to use the spreadsheet, so make sure there is room for expansion. A good way of doing so is to make use of the worksheets feature, whereby you can have different types of information on separate sheets. For example, you could have the raw data on sheet 1, and a summary of it on sheet 2.

Automate as much as you can

Remember the principle of right first time. The spreadsheet can fetch data from one place to another, and you can use the IF function to give grades based on the marks awarded.

Don't underestimate the power of the spreadsheet

There are hundreds of built-in formulae in modern spreadsheets, and you can combine them in all sorts of ways. Even calculations like standard deviation can be carried out automatically through a built-in formula.

Name cell references

Although it is faster to enter formulae by clicking on the cells involved, this gives you formulae like =G7-B7. It is better to name the cells involved, so that you get =ActualGrade-PredictedGrade. This is easier to read, and makes trouble-shooting easier.

CAPITATION

It goes without saying that Heads of Department (HoDs) will want to keep a record of how much they've spent, and the items on which they've spent it. However, it is possible to go beyond these basics and create a computer-based system of real usefulness without too much extra work.

A simple capitation system

It is possible to create a complete system which will not only keep track of what you've been spending money on but also produce word processed reports at the press of a button. This, though, requires some rather involved techniques. A compromise is to use a belt and braces approach will do the job without involving a great deal of technical expertise. In fact, the two suggestions here are really two stages of one solution, but the second stage is optional. These stages are:

— Stage 1: Create a capitation spreadsheet

— Stage 2: Create a summary report in your word processor based on the data in the spreadsheet.

The spreadsheet

Setting up the spreadsheet is a little time-consuming, but is worth the effort. The first thing to do is create a table of products and codes somewhere in your spreadsheet. You can make up the codes yourself.

The Lookup Function

The lookup function takes several forms. This spreadsheet uses the Vertical Lookup function, usually called vlookup.

The numbers in the first column are made up. The idea is to have sets of numbers for paper, for pens, exercise books, text books and so on. This system enables you to use the spreadsheet to calculate how much money you spend on paper, how much on pens, etc. Using a 3-figure code enables you to insert more sub-categories easily.

In the main body of your spreadsheet you use a lookup formula to insert the information. For example, to insert Lined A4 paper you just enter the code, 101, and the spreadsheet will insert the rest of the information automatically.

CERTIFICATING PUPIL ACHIEVEMENT

If pupils/students are achieving well, you'll probably want to let them know that their efforts are appreciated. Here are a few things to consider:

Producing the certificates

The most effective way of creating certificates is to create a template in a word processor or desktop publisher, and then use that as the basis for creating all future certificates.

You may find that your word processor already has a certificate or award template which is more or less suitable for your needs. You can always open the template as a document, make any necessary adjustments, and then save it as a template again. If you use a program which, like Microsoft Word, has a procedure whereby a certificate is produced by the program based on your responses to a series of questions (in Microsoft products these are called "wizards"), create the certificate, make the required amendments, and then save it as a template.

Recording certification

You will probably want to keep a record of who has been given a certificate, and for what, and when.

Informing others

Here is a method which relies on mail-merging:

— Create a document consisting of the names of pupils to be accredited, and why.

— Create a certificate based on the template. Make this the basis of a mail-merged document linked to the document called "Names".

— In the space reserved for the student's name, insert the field Name in the Names document, while in the space reserved for the reason for the award insert the field called Reason in the Names document.

— Carry out the merge procedure.

— Create a letter to parents. Make this the basis of a mail-merged document linked to the document called "Names"

— In the space reserved for the student's name, insert the field Name in the Names document, while in the space reserved for the reason for the award insert the field called Reason in the Names document.

MAINTAINING YOUR CV

Your INSET record

It's a good idea to maintain a separate database of your training (INSET), because you can amend it and add to it without taking the risk of accidentally deleting part of your CV! This "database" can be in the form of a spreadsheet or a table in your word processor.

Layout

The aspect of CVs that causes many people problems is the layout. The easiest way of laying out the document is to use a table, rather than tabs, with an invisible border. Using a table means that you can easily line up columns, move whole blocks of text at once simply by widening the column or making it narrower and be certain the document is going to print out properly.

EXAMINATION ENTRY & ANALYSIS

Here is a summary of the process involved:

— The Examination Board sends the school or college the syllabus identity codes, plus details of examination components and their deadlines.

— The school or college sends the Examination Board a list of candidates, together with their individual numbers and the examinations for which they are being entered.

— The Examination Board sends the examination results to the school or college.

Disadvantages of using a paper-based approach

— It is time-consuming

— Often, the same data has to be entered by different people, such as students' names. This goes against the principle of right first time

— The analysis of the results is very tedious

Advantages of using a computer, and especially Electronic Data Exchange (EDI)

— Using a computer enables you to use an optical mark reader (OMR) to input data quickly

— Data transfer via EDI is very fast and accurate

— There are fewer opportunities for errors, because data is only entered once

— EDI can be set up to work in the middle of the night, when there are no other demands on the computer system, and when there is least likelihood of someone breaking the connection

— The computer can detect exam timetable clashes immediately.

Examination analysis

A good computer program can analyse examination results extremely quickly, and in numerous ways, and can print reports on the results very soon after they have arrived.

KEEPING TRACK OF HOMEWORK

Keeping a diary of homework you've set your classes is not only a good idea from the point of view of knowing what the students should be handing in for marking, but also gives you an overview of the homework that you have set over time or between different groups. Moreover, it can act as independent "evidence" that you've actually set homework, should anyone enquire.

Create a table

The easiest way to keep track of homework, and to be able to organise the data in different ways, is to create a table. You can either do this in a word processor, or in a spreadsheet. The table should consist of the following headings:

— Group
— Topic
— Homework set
— Date set
— Completion date
— (optional) Follow-up work/Comments

Word processor or spreadsheet?

The advantage of a word processor is that it is quick and easy to use. Also, by creating a table you can easily sort the data by group, date set, topic and so on. In a sense, though, a spreadsheet is even easier to use because:

— The table is already set up for you, which can save you quite a bit of time
— You can use the spreadsheet as a database, enabling you to look up the homework you set between the 10th and the 17th May, say
— The spreadsheet "understands" dates.

A student homework record

You may wish to keep a record of the homework you've set, and the response of individual students, such as the mark awarded or even whether or not it was completed.

Although you can do this in a fairly simple way using a spreadsheet or a word processor, you can end up entering a lot of data more than once, or using a coding system which could soon get out of hand. This is because for each student you will need to keep a table showing the following:

— Student's name

— Student's group

— Topic

— Homework set

— Date set

— Date to be handed in

— Date handed in

— Completed?

— Mark/Grade awarded

As you can see, much of the information required is the same as mentioned earlier, and will be repeated for each student. A better approach would therefore be to use a relational database management system (RDBMS). This would consist of tables which link up to each other. In this example, the tables required would be as shown in the screenshot.

The RDBMS could then be configured in such a way that you could enter the homework in one table, enter the students' names (or import them) into another table, and the homework would be assigned to the students automatically. You would not have to enter the details of any homework or student more than once.

INFORMING PEOPLE

In school or college, a large number of people needs to be kept informed or reminded of various events. Quite often, several people have to be informed of the same event, and a record has to be kept of who has been informed of what. For example, if you give a detention to a pupil, a certain number of records may be generated:

— Detention slip to pupil.

— Your own record of the detention.

— A note to the pupils' parents informing them of the detention.

— A note to the pupil's form teacher.

— A note to the pupil's Head of Year.

A computer could be used to do most of the work involved in this process. Options you may wish to consider include:

— Enter the data once, and send it to all the parties concerned using mail-merging techniques.

— Enter the data onto electronic forms, because many of the options can be semi-automated through the use of buttons and drop-down menus. The data can then be used for mail-merging.

Here, as in many other contexts, the most important considerations are that data should need to be entered only once, and it should not be time-consuming to do so. There is an added benefit of using a computer system, which is that you can easily generate data on how many times a particular pupil has been in detention, what the most common reason for detention has been, and so on.

INSET RECORDS

Both individual teachers and Heads of Department need to keep track of the courses staff attend. In the case of the individual teacher, this information is usually required on application forms. For the Head of Department, it is important to have an overall idea of who has attended what, in order to make sure there is a good balance of skills in the department, and that individuals are getting the professional development to which they are entitled.

The easiest method of keeping track is to start a table in a word-processed document or start a spreadsheet. It must include details, for each individual, of:

— Course title

— Course topic

— Organiser

— Dates attended

The reason a table or spreadsheet is a good idea is that it is easy to get it started (databases can be complicated), and it makes the data easy to sort and analyse.

LESSON PLANS AND OTHER DEPARTMENT RECORDS

There are several benefits from using computers at departmental level:

— Departmental documentation

— Examination analysis

— Finding documents

Departmental documentation

Create templates for meeting agenda, minutes, lesson plans and other documents. This not only saves time but also creates an impression of consistency and cohesiveness across the department. In the case of lesson plan templates it also helps to ensure that certain points are addressed by all members of staff. If there is a school or college template, it becomes much easier for the senior management team and others to find what they are looking for in a number of departments, and it gives outsiders the impression of there being a whole-school or college approach to the curriculum.

Examination analysis

Rather than have each member of staff carry out their own analysis of examination results which the head of department then has to collate, it makes more sense for them to enter the marks into a departmental spreadsheet straight away. Even if a different file is given to each department, if they are all basically the same collating the results will be painless and relatively quick.

Finding documents

Having a well-structured filing system on the school or college network can make it very easy to locate documents. For example, if you need to look at the minutes of the meeting in which the college annexe was discussed, it should take only a few seconds to find that document. It may be worth investing in document management software.

MAINTAINING LISTS

In the average school or college, a great deal of data is held centrally about each pupil or student. It is therefore self-evident that if anyone has to write out lists of names for any reason, the system is not being used properly.

The stages involved in producing a list

There are three stages involved in the production or updating of lists:

— Enter or amend the data

— Produce a report

— Distribute the report

Enter or amend the data

Entering data can sometimes be done by electronic means, such as with an optical mark reader (OMR). Amending data can be done very quickly using a feature known as an update query, if you are using a database system like Access. If the program doesn't have this facility, you can still carry out the task fairly quickly using the Search and Replace feature.

Produce a report

The software used will normally have a few pre-configured reports, but you will almost certainly be able to configure your own (if not, buy different software).

Distribute the report

Distribute the report to interested parties, or display it on a noticeboard. If it is distributed electronically, either on disk or via an intranet, heads of department and others can use the data in ways useful to their departments. Distributing the report on paper only can lead to more (unnecessary) work.

MANAGING MEETINGS

There are three aspects of managing meetings, if we consider the subject in its broadest sense. These are:

— Arranging the meetings

— Producing the documentation for meetings, such as the Agenda and Minutes

— Keeping track of progress being made on allocated tasks between meetings.

Arranging meetings

It can be quite difficult to arrange a meeting between people who have many commitments and are always busy. One solution, which many schools and colleges have adopted, is to have a regular meeting slot on the timetable for different groups of people, such as HoDs or Senior Management. While there are advantages and disadvantages of this approach, it does not solve the problem of calling a non-routine meeting. There are a couple of computer-based solutions available. These can be classified as automated scheduling and manual scheduling.

Automated scheduling

What happens is that you "tell" the program that you want to call a meeting, and who is to be invited. The software will then look through every invitee's electronic diary and suggest the best time for a meeting. The software can even be set up to notify everyone of the meeting by internal electronic mail.

Manual scheduling

This works on the same lines as automated scheduling, except that a human being rather than a computer does the work. In this approach, what happens is that people enter details of their meetings in a common file. This could be a spreadsheet, suitably set out. In fact, to save time and also to increase the likelihood of people entering details of their meetings, they could be asked merely to place an X in each time slot when they have a meeting. Alternatively, staff could be asked to give details of their meetings to the administrative assistants, who could then enter them on the system.

Documentation

This is extremely easy to produce. All you need to do is to create templates in your word processor. Then, whenever you need to produce an Agenda or set of Minutes, you merely start a new document and select the appropriate template. On the template you can place all the text you will need, such as the school logo (which can be scanned in using a flatbed or hand-held scanner, either of which is very inexpensive these days), text such as "Minutes" and so on. Don't forget that you can also set up the margins, font style and type, and just about every other aspect of the document.

In most word processors, in order to make use of the template you select File-New and then choose the template from a list.

Automated templates

It is possible to automate some of the aspects of producing an Agenda or a set of Minutes through the use of macros. For example, you could get the document to prompt you for such details as the date of the meeting or the people from whom apologies have been received. But even without such enhancements, the template is a very powerful tool. It could, for example, be made available to all staff – via the curriculum network if staff don't have access to the admin network. With minor modifications, the same basic template could be used by all departments. This helps to reinforce a whole-school or college outlook. It also saves many people a great deal of time.

Keeping track of progress

Many Minutes include action details which specify what is to be done, who is responsible for ensuring that it does get done, and when it is to be done by. Not only managers, but also the responsible people themselves, need to keep track of their progress and to plan their activities accordingly.

For large projects you could use Project Management programs. These ask you for details such as what needs to be achieved, and in what order (some things cannot be done until certain conditions have been satisfied), and what resources are available. The software will then work out what has to be done by when. It will enable you to see what still needs to be done at any given stage, who is responsible for what, and other data.It is possible to create your own project management program using either a programming language or a relational management database system. This is, however, both complicated and time-consuming.

MAINTAINING A DEPARTMENTAL DEVELOPMENT PLAN

Like so many other topics covered here, the computerised version of a departmental development plan can be as simple or as complex as you want it to be. Here we consider three options:

— simple development plan

— complex development plan and

— compromise between the two

A simple development plan

A simple development plan comprises three columns with the following headings:

— Action to be taken

— Person responsible

— Date to be completed

Clearly, you could produce this as a document in your word processor. However, it would be a good idea to produce it either in the form of a table or to produce it using a spreadsheet.

A complex development plan

You may want to adopt a rather more precise approach to development planning, in which case you might consider project software. This type of program enables you to specify the resources at your disposal, including time and personnel, the main objectives to be achieved, the prerequisites of achieving those objectives and so on.

What you end up with is a complete plan showing who needs to do what by when. In other words, the program will calculate, based on the information you supply, that in order to, say, run a successful INSET session in May you will need to have started the booklet for it by January 16th.

Project software is therefore very good when your end goal is very much dependent upon a number of interim stages, or sub-objectives, being achieved first, and where different sub-objectives will take different amounts of resources to achieve. It can, however, take a long time and a lot of thought to set up a project, and only you can decide whether the goal under consideration is worth it or not.

A compromise solution

There is a kind of half-way house between these two approaches. If you create your development plan in a spreadsheet, you can create a macro which will, say, highlight all those cells in which today's date is greater than the date of uncompleted task. That will give you instant feedback on overdue items. You could have the macro shade uncompleted but not overdue items in a different colour.

MAINTAINING A DIARY

There are two main uses for diaries:

— for an individual to note the date of meetings and

— for groups of people to arrange meetings.

Although in many respects an electronic diary is not as convenient as a pocket or desk diary, it does have one or two advantages, as we'll see.

Diaries for individual use are called Personal Information Managers (PIMs) while diaries for group use are called Schedulers.

Both PIMs and Schedulers usually consist of a number of sections, including:

— address book

— diary

— year planner

— notebook

— alarm/reminder.

A good program will also let you add your own sections, perhaps based on existing sections. For example, you may be able to create a "yellow pages" address section so that you can keep business and personal contacts separate from each other.

PIMs

A good PIM will let you enter a meeting in the diary and link the entry to names of people in the address book and to entries in the notebook. The entry will also automatically be made in the year planner.

So you could look in your year planner, and double-click on a date. This will take you into the diary view, where you will see that the meeting is due to start at 10 am, and that there are some notes about the meeting. You click on the link to the notebook, where you see links to people in the address book. Clicking on one of these links enables you to contact one of the other people in order to clarify one or two points. In fact, the PIM may even dial the number for you; it should certainly enable you to keep track of the phone calls you make.

Schedulers

These are similar to PIMs but they have an important extra function. When used over a network they can:

— scan the diaries of everyone in a certain group to find out the next time everyone is free

— enter the meeting in everyone's diary

— send everyone an email message informing them of the meeting.

So you can see that electronic diaries can be extremely useful, but they do rely on everyone entering the relevant data, and this can sometimes be inconvenient. If you wish to keep a paper diary as well, the electronic version will usually allow you to print off notes, entries and contact details in the format of your choice.

POLICY MANAGEMENT

We can distinguish between the procedural and the substantive aspects of policies. It is the procedural aspects which are dealt with here, although you will probably have to amend the procedure for different policies. Nevertheless, there are certain generic aspects of policies and policy management with which a computer can assist.

Drafting policies

Even at the earliest draft stages, use a word processor rather than pencil and paper, because a good word processor enables you to rearrange and view the material in different ways. In particular you can make use of the following features:

- Outlining
- Moving text
- Highlighting
- Revision mode
- Versions.

Outlining

This enables you to show only the headings, rather than the text below the headings. It also enables you to move whole chunks of text around simply by moving the heading. In order for this feature to work, you must find out about and make use of your word processor's heading or paragraph style feature.

Moving text

You can reorder lists and paragraphs or just sentences or single words, either through a keyboard shortcut, cut/copy and paste or drag and drop.

Highlighting

Some word processors now have a highlighting feature which works in the same way as ordinary highlighter pens. Also, if the document is being developed by several people, each person can have their own highlighter colour.

Revision mode

This enables you to make changes to text without making the changes permanent right away. Thus, if you delete something, it does not disappear from the screen, it has a line put through it. It will only disappear if you accept the change. You can use this feature to make changes to a document which you, or someone else if you are not the author, can choose to accept or reject.

Versions

If you make changes to a document, or if several people are going to comment on the document, you can save each person's version under the same file name but a different version number. If your word processor does not have this feature, you can achieve a similar outcome by saving the document under different names.

Automatically updating common elements

Most policies will have some common elements, such as the School or College Development Plan, demographic details and so on. If you store these details in a separate document, all you have to do is reference the document, not type it again. In the paper version of your policy, you have a choice of inserting the details document as a file, or linking or embedding the details document in your policy document. If you link the document, any time you update the details document, your policy documents will be automatically updated the next time you open them. In the on-line or intranet version, you can have hypertext links to the common elements.

Minimal use of computers

If your establishment does not have computers widely available for staff use, you can still make the secretary's life easier by using a printed template for policies, or at least a set format. This will minimise the amount of time the secretary has to think about things like layout.

As well as a template, it would also be useful to have a style sheet. This sets out the fonts to be used, margins and so on. It helps to make all documents have a similar look, and substantially cuts down on the amount of time spent thinking about what font to use, whether to have semi-colons at the end of bullet points, and so on.

Availability

Policies are only policies in the true sense of the word if they are put into practice, and for this to happen they must be generally available. The most effective way of achieving this is by posting them on the school or college intranet, which is one of the things you might consider as your way of participating in the National Grid for Learning.

Alternatively, post them on your internet site, perhaps passwording the pages so as to restrict access to staff as far as possible. If neither of these is possible, they should be placed in an easily-accessible area on the school or college network.

These do not replace paper-based systems, but they do help to ensure that should anyone wish to refer to a policy, it will be only a few mouse clicks away. It also makes it easier for staff to print out sections for displaying in their teaching areas, should they wish to do so.

PROJECT MANAGEMENT

It is a program designed to help you plan, manage and keep track of projects. Here we consider the following:

— What's the problem?

— What project software does

— Is project software necessary for a school or college?

What's the problem?

Most projects are difficult to plan or keep track of because the end task or tasks usually cannot be completed until certain other tasks have been completed. Thus, once you've set a deadline for the completion of the final task, you have to work out when the sub-task need to be completed by in order to ensure that the final deadline is met. It is highly unlikely that all of the sub-tasks will take the same length of time to complete, and so you end up with several tasks all coming to fruition at different times.

At the same time, you have only finite resources of labour and time, and you have to ensure that these are allocated in the most efficient way. It's a bit like cooking a meal. You have various ingredients, and they all have to be processed in a different way in order to contribute in the best way to the final result. These different processes all take different lengths of time to complete, and it is important to avoid starting any of them either too early or too late.

What project software does

Project software helps you to think through the processes in a logical manner. The program will summarise which resources have been allocated to which tasks. It will also produce a timeline showing what has to be completed by when and by whom. Thus it will provide a visual check on what should be happening at any particular point in time.

Is it necessary?

No. You could use a scheduling program instead, or just rely on pen and paper. However, project software will assist you in managing resources and deadlines more easily than these alternatives.

PUBLICITY & IMAGE

It is often the case that the first impression "outsiders" have of a school or college is its documentation, such as the Prospectus, or what it reads about in the local press. Therefore attention to detail in these areas could pay dividends in the long run. In this section we look at the following:

— Style consistency

— Style sheets

— Press releases

Style consistency

The single most important consideration is consistency of style. All documentation which emanates from the institution, whether it be a press release or a letter to parents, should look the same. In fact, as far as possible all internal documentation should have the same or similar appearance too.

This is known as a "house style". Having a house style achieves several things:

— It helps to give the school or college a recognisable identity
— It indicates that you consider the appearance of documentation to be important
— It saves individuals having to make decisions about the style of their documents.

Use a style sheet

A good approach to this is to develop a house style sheet and ask all staff to use it as a basis for their documents. The style sheet should be developed by, or in co-operation with, someone who understands principles of design. It covers paragraph styles, including fonts, spacing before and after paragraphs and so on, and margins.

The house style should also be incorporated into all the templates used, to make it easier for staff to follow the guidelines. The templates could have the school or college logo already imported into it, and a space could be designated for departmental logos or slogans, if appropriate.

Placeholder text and graphics could be included too. This is text and graphics which are there purely to be replaced by the user's own text and graphics. It saves the user having to worry about design, or about how to achieve a certain effect.

The easier it is to use a template to produce good-looking documents, the more likely people are to want to use them.

Press releases

As well as developing a rapport with local reporters in order to be able to telephone them with news about the school or college, you may also want to make sure you send them press releases on a regular basis. It would be a good idea to set up a template for this in your word processor, or use a template supplied with the program. That would help to ensure consistency of appearance. The press release should include details of who to contact, and how, a headline, and a few paragraphs of text. The first paragraph should state the bare facts. The second paragraph should enlarge on the facts, perhaps providing some background or wider perspective. The third paragraph should end with a quote from the Head or Principal, or at least a member of the Senior Management Team.

RECORDS OF ACHIEVEMENT

This is an area in which the student has to be involved in the actual process of creating the document. It is not, therefore, a simple matter of looking at technical solutions. The real problem is this: how do you involve 200 pupils in the creation of an individual document without needing three years to do so?

Types of program available

There are two basic types of commercial program available: those which are designed to be used to process the data centrally, and those which are designed for use by individual students. Some of the programs are designed to be used as part of an administration software suite, while others are designed as stand-alone programs. Some of the stand-alone programs have a wider brief than just records of achievement, such as helping students to make career decisions.

Must you buy a program?

No. You can develop your own "program" using a word processor. You will need to reproduce the different records of achievement pages as templates or electronic forms.

General considerations

The main advantage of the "central" programs is that they can pull in most of the data from other modules, such as name, subjects taken, grades attained, and so forth – although the student will still have to write their personal statement.

The main advantage of the student-oriented programs is that they are entirely personal to the student. Also, there is less pressure on the central admin facilities when printing out the records of achievement.

The disadvantages of the student-oriented software, however, are that in practice it is extremely difficult for all students to gain adequate access to the computer system. Also, there is little central control over spelling and grammar.

Perhaps a compromise would be to use a commercial program for the bulk of the data, and your own word processed templates for the student statement only.

Whichever approach you use, printing is a big issue because each page of the record of achievement is different. Therefore it is not possible to print off a whole batch of records of achievement – unless you print a whole lot of first pages, followed by all the other pages in turn, and then collate them afterwards.

REGISTRATION

We can think of registration as having two distinct phases: data collection and data analysis. The time-honoured method of registering pupils or students is perfectly OK as far as collecting the data is concerned, but it does not lend itself to very efficient data analysis.

Computerised registration systems excel in the analysis of the data. As well as being able to calculate percentage attendance rates for all pupils in a matter of seconds, as opposed to having form teachers spending hours on the same task, they can also tell you that Fred Bloggs of 11C has been absent at exactly the same times as Leanne Soap from 10B for the past three months – something which you may not have picked up on using the traditional system.

Broadly speaking, there are four electronic means of registration. These are, in increasing order of sophistication:

— Optical mark readers

— Bar coding

— EARS

— Swipe cards

Optical Mark Readers

This is very similar to the usual method of marking the register. In fact, as far as the teacher is concerned, it is exactly the same. However, when the register, which consists of a single sheet of paper for that day or lesson, has been taken, it is then sent to the school or college office, where it is scanned into the computer via a device called an optical mark reader (OMR).

Advantages of OMR

The OMR system has the following advantages:

— It is very similar to the traditional system, and so requires relatively little staff training

— Various statistics can be generated very quickly

— It transfers data analysis from teachers to the computer system.

Disadvantages of OMR

It has the following disadvantages:

— There will still need to be some staff training in completing the registers, because marks made on the register may be ignored if not made properly, and extraneous marks may be read

— A system will need to be established whereby the registers are processed as soon as possible after registration

— The cost of the registers can be quite high – between 4p and 8p per sheet at the time of writing

— The amount of paper generated is quite phenomenal, especially if the register is taken in each lesson as well as at the beginning of each morning and afternoon, as it would be in a college

— It may be necessary to keep all of the paper records in case the computer system "goes down" or the data gets lost – otherwise, what would you present in court if it came to it? However, an overload of paper can be avoided by printing out weekly and half-termly absent reports for form teachers.

Bar coding

In this approach, the teacher marks the register in the usual herringbone style. Each pupil is assigned a bar code, which is printed next to his or her name on the register. The completed register is sent to the school office, where a member of the administrative staff uses a bar code reader to scan in pupils marked absent: the system assumes that an unread bar code indicates that the child is present.

Advantages of Bar coding

The main advantage of bar coding over OMR is:

— It is probably more reliable when it comes to transferring the data from the register to the school's computer system, because it "looks at" a pre-printed bar code rather than the register itself.

Disadvantages of BAR CODING

The main disadvantage of bar coding over OMR is:

— It is a fiddly business scanning in some pupils but not others, and one that would seem to be quite prone to human error.

EARS

This is the Electronic Attendance Registration System. Each teacher is issued with a kind of laptop computer on which s/he takes the register. The data is then transmitted to a computer in the school office, where it is held for processing.

Advantages of EARS

The EARS approach has the following advantages

- It is entirely paperless
- You can register every lesson very easily
- There is an option for instant viewing of an individual's history of class or form registration;
- You can produce absence lists immediately from central computer.

Disadvantages of EARS

The EARS approach has the following disadvantages:

- Registration folders cannot be used for anything else at present, but this may change in the future
- The initial cost is quite high: approximately £35,000 for a school with 70 full-time teachers
- Despite assurances by the suppliers, the system is potentially very vulnerable to vandalism.

Swipe cards

In this approach, pupils swipe a card into a card reader as they enter the school and, if you like, as they enter classrooms too. The cards can be used for other purposes too, such as taking out library books and paying for school meals. The form tutor is given a list of pupils present, and registration time can be either reduced or used for other things.

Advantages of swipe cards

Swipe cards have the following advantages:

— Registration time can be used for something more educationally useful than taking the register.

— Pupils are given some "real world" responsibility and experience.

Disadvantages of swipe cards

Swipe cards have the following disadvantages:

— There can be bottlenecks at the card reader points

— The data generated has not yet been tested in court: given that pupils can register each other, is the data reliable?

— The form tutor or teacher still has to do a visual check – ie take the register, in effect – to see if the names on the register tally with the students in the classroom

— The cost is extremely high.

As in every other field of human endeavour, introducing computerised methods has enormous potential benefits, but there is also a potential cost in terms of the consequences of losing data. This is an area that should not be overlooked, and a school or college will want to consider ways of archiving paper-based records, and not relying exclusively on the computer system.

REPORTING TO PARENTS

Many people do not like the idea of computerised reporting systems because they feel that they are too impersonal. This is not necessarily true, but in any case there are several tasks that a computer can be used for in order to save valuable staff time:

Types of report

- Headed reports
- Full reports
- Information letters

Headed reports

These are reports which have details like the student's name, group and subject automatically entered at the top, leaving the tutor to enter the actual comments by hand. Heading the reports in this way can save a considerable amount of time.

Full reports

These are reports which are fully completed by computer, and may involve the use of statement banks.

Information letters

If you maintain marks and grades on a computer system, periodic letters can be sent home to parents informing them of their child's progress. You can use mail-merging techniques to ensure that these letters can be generated with almost no extra effort on your part.

SCHEDULING & CONTACT MANAGEMENT

Although the underlying rationale of scheduling and contact management programs are different, their functions do overlap. They are worth considering in order to improve the efficiency of key individuals and groups within an educational institution.

Scheduling programs

These can fix up meetings between busy people by looking at their diaries and identifying a mutually convenient date and time. In addition, these programs can be used to:

— keep track of phone calls

— keep notes on meetings

— exchange notes between members of the team

— exchange files between members of the team

Contact Management programs

These were designed originally for use by salespeople. They enable you to:

— keep a list of contacts, with their addresses and phone numbers

— keep notes on each one

— keep track of phone calls

— keep notes on phone calls

— produce personalised letters based on notes made about a phone conversation

This type of program is intended more for dealing with external contacts than internal ones, but many of them can be configured to arrange meetings just like scheduling programs. If you have a lot of external contacts, this type of program may be worth considering, either instead of or, most likely, as well as scheduling software.

SPECIAL EDUCATIONAL NEEDS

The Code of Practice may be simplified, and therefore made more manageable, soon. In terms of a process, going through the requirements of the Code of Practice is similar to that for organising trips.

The word processor as a database

At each stage of the process, a form of some description will have to be completed. Set up the forms as templates on the computer network, and call them Stage1, Stage2 and so on. (You could also have one called IEP). You could set up a system whereby the names of pupils identified in Stage 1 will be stored in another document as a database. Then subsequent forms could be linked by mail-merging techniques to this database. Keeping a database in this way will not be as efficient as keeping a "proper" relational database management system, but it would work OK and be relatively easy to set up. You will need a macro which runs whenever a new document is created with one of the templates. The syntax will differ between different programs, but the algorithm is as follows:

— When you start a document based on the Stage 1 template, a dialog box pops up asking you for the pupils' details – name, form and today's date.

— Your replies are stored as variables. These variables are then inserted into pre-designated places in the new document.

— The database document is then opened.

— Then the data you've entered in the dialog box is entered into the database.

— The document is saved and closed.

— Other templates could be linked to the database document as mail-merged documents. Macros embedded in them could ask for additional information, some of which might be entered into another document and saved as an IEP.

The data document in the word processor could be sorted and searched like any database using the mail merge search options. Alternatively, it could be exported into a database program and searched and sorted there.

STAFF APPRAISAL

Running a staff appraisal involves three main processes:

— Matching up appraisers and appraisees

— Completing documentation
— Keeping track of progress.

Matching up appraisers and appraisees

This is usually done by mutual consent. If necessary, the process can be computerised by using a spreadsheet. The purpose of the spreadsheet would be to check that the appraiser is of an equal or higher level than the appraisee.

Completing documentation

A good way of ensuring that the correct documentation is completed is to make sure that all the relevant templates are on the network system. To ensure that it is completed in the correct sequence, try the solution suggested for school trips.

Keeping track of progress

It would be a good idea to set up a directory structure along these lines on the school administration system:

```
C:
    staff
        appraisal
            badger
            bloggs
            bruton
```

and so on. You could then keep track of who is at what stage of the process simply by looking in the relevant directory.

TARGET-SETTING

Whatever the level at which the target-setting is being done, there are certain generic ways in which a computer can help make the process of checking progress easier. What is required is an easy way of checking outcomes against intentions.

A simple solution

The simplest solution is to use a word processor and produce a template or document for all concerned to use.

A dynamic solution

You could use a scheduling or project management program to help manage targets and to check progress. For an individual or small department, an ordinary Personal Information Manager may be adequate.

You could also design your own table in a spreadsheet which would help you keep track of how you were meeting your targets. The table might look like the one above, but with the addition of two columns: Days remaining to the completion date, and an evaluation of the situation.

You would need to insert a formula to calculate the number of days remaining to the completion date. The evaluation column would contain an IF formula which will tell you at a glance if you have run out of time, or are about to run out of time. This may sound somewhat pointless, but when you are juggling several different targets, even the simplest of tools can help.

TIMETABLING

For a very large department or the whole school or college, a timetabling program is essential because it enables you to see the effects on the whole picture of changing just one or two variables. However, it is important to understand that timetabling programs just do number-crunching. They can make everything fit, but whether it's a good fit in educational or administrative terms is something that a computer cannot say.

A good timetabling program will have an interactive mode, which allows you to choose from a number of suggested solutions and modify them, rather than merely present you with an "ideal" solution. The software should make it easy to prevent excessive movement of staff or pupils, or putting someone in two classes at once. Many timetabling programs nowadays can be used, either on their own or in conjunction with other programs, to create individual student timetables. In the case of a department, consider the ideas suggested in Allocating staff to teaching groups.

ORGANISING TRIPS

As you know, organising a trip is fraught with difficulties. You need to ensure that all the necessary forms have been completed in good time. The computer can facilitate a simple yet effective solution. All you need is a word processor and, possibly, a scanner.

The word processor solution

The word processor solution is very simple. It relies on the fact that, in order to organise a successful school or college trip, you must process a number of documents, usually in a particular order.

Rather than having only a set of complicated guidelines which can be mislaid, why not make all of the necessary documents available at the click of a mouse button in the school's word processor?

In order to achieve this, you may need to scan in certain documents, such as LEA insurance forms. The way this solution would operate in practice would be as follows.

The person organising the trip would open a document called TRIPS. This document would contain either a list of "live links" to other documents, or just one live link to the next document.

The advantage of having just one live link in each document is that the user is taken automatically through the documents in the correct sequence. The disadvantage is that you do not get a sense of where you are in the process. However, that could be overcome by having extra information in each document.

All necessary documents can be included in this system: a template for creating the initial information in order to gauge likely student numbers, insurance forms, student list and deposits received, parental permission letters and so on.

VISITOR TRACKING

Apart from taking physical measures, such as limiting the number of entrances to the site, what can you do to improve security with respect to visitors? In other words, how can you make sure that people who shouldn't be on site are spotted quickly?

Minimum measures

These do not require a computer. They consist of:

— Getting visitors to sign in

— Giving them a badge with their name on.

This latter could be greatly improved by putting the date and time of the visit on the badge, so that it cannot be re-used.

How a computer can help

There is software available to help you keep track of visitors. This software, generally speaking, will:

— Print out a personalised badge with details of the date, time and expected duration of the visit as well as the visitor's name

— Maintain a database of who visited whom, and when

— Enable you to scan in photographs of regular visitors so that you can produce permanent badges for them.

It is possible that the educational software suite you use has a visitor tracking module, so ask your supplier or support company about it.

13

Ensuring Safe Use of the Internet

"'Cyberspace,' the 'Web,' the 'Net,' the 'Information Highway'" —Whatever it's called, millions of people are now going online to exchange electronic mail, surf the World Wide Web, post and read messages in newsgroups (sometimes called bulletin boards), and participate in chat groups and many other online activities.

There are a number of ways to get online. In addition to major commercial online services, there are thousands of Internet Service Providers (ISPs) that provide Internet access. Telephone companies, cable TV companies, and even some local newspapers offer Internet access, usually for a monthly fee. Although most people use personal computers to get online, it's now possible to purchase a special adapter that allows you to access the Internet from a TV set.

ISPs and online services generally do everything they can to provide their subscribers with an enjoyable, safe, and rewarding online experience, but it's not possible for these companies to police everyone who uses their service anymore than a local government can control the behavior of its citizens. Besides, once you're connected to the Internet, you're able to exchange information with people who are signed on with other ISPs and online services. The Internet is a vast global network of networks that's not governed by any company or government. Anyone in the world — companies, governments, organizations, and individuals — can publish material on the Internet. An ISP links you to these sites, but it can't control what is on them. It's up to individuals to make sure that they behave in a way that's safe and appropriate.

The vast array of services that you currently find online is constantly growing. Reference information such as news, weather, sports, stock quotes, movie reviews, encyclopedias, and airline fares are readily available online. Users can conduct transactions such as trading stocks, making travel reservations, banking, and shopping online. You can find information about your local schools and government, read an out-of-town newspaper, or obtain vital health information.

Millions of people communicate through electronic mail (E-mail) with family and friends around the world. Others use the public message board chat areas to make new friends who share common interests. You can even use the Internet to watch video and listen to audio programs produced by major media companies, businesses, organizations, and even individuals. As an educational and entertainment tool users can learn about virtually any topic, visit a museum, take a college course, or play an endless number of computer games with other users or against the computer itself.

Most people who go online have mainly positive experiences. But, like any endeavor — traveling, cooking, or attending school — there are some risks. The online world, like the rest of society, is made up of a wide array of people. Most are decent and respectful, but some may be rude, obnoxious, insulting, or even mean and exploitative. Children get a lot of benefit from being online, but they can also be targets of crime and exploitation in this as in any other environment. Trusting, curious, and anxious to explore this new world and the relationships it brings, children need parental supervision and common-sense advice on how to be sure that their experiences in "cyberspace" are happy, healthy, and productive.

Although there have been some highly publicized cases of abuse involving the Internet and online services, reported cases are relatively infrequent. Of course, like most crimes against children, many cases go unreported, especially if the child is engaged in an activity that he or she does not want to discuss with a parent.

The fact that crimes are being committed online, however, is *not* a reason to avoid using these services. To tell children to stop using these services would be like telling them to forgo attending school because students are sometimes victimized there.

A better strategy would be to instruct children about both the benefits and dangers of cyberspace and for them to learn how to be "street smart" in order to better safeguard themselves in any potentially dangerous situation.

WHAT ARE THE RISKS?

There are a few risks for children who use the Internet or online services. Teenagers are particularly at risk because they often use the computer unsupervised and because they are more likely than younger children to participate in online discussions regarding companionship, relationships, or sexual activity.

Some risks are:

— *Exposure to Inappropriate Material*: One risk is that a child may be exposed to inappropriate material that is sexual, hateful, or violent in nature, or encourages activities that are dangerous or illegal.

— *Physical Molestation*: Another risk is that, while online, a child might provide information or arrange an encounter that could risk his or her safety or the safety of other family members. In a few cases, pedophiles have used E-mail, bulletin boards, and chat areas to gain a child's confidence and then arrange s face-to-face meeting.

— *Harassment:* A third risk is that a child might encounter E-mail or chat/bulletin board messages that are harassing, demeaning, or belligerent.

— *Legal and Financial:* There is also the risk that a child could do something that has negative legal or financial consequences such as giving out a parent's credit card number or doing something that violates another person's rights. Legal issues aside, children should be taught good "netiquette" which means to avoid being rude, mean, or inconsiderate.

Internet Crimes Against Children

New computer technology presents complex challenges for law enforcement agencies and victim service providers. These professionals must protect Internet users as they conduct investigations, secure evidence, identify and apprehend offenders, and help child victims and their families. Based on the knowledge and experience of those working with child victims, this Bulletin focuses attention on child victims of Internet-based crimes, highlighting the challenges for law enforcement personnel and victim service providers, examining who the child victims are, and determining how best to respond to these victims' needs and the needs of their families.

The growth of technology has changed our lives dramatically. Computers were viewed as a luxury or even an extravagance 30 years ago. We relied on television, newspapers, and radio as primary sources of news and information. Cables, modems, and online services were virtually nonexistent.

Today, computers are prevalent in businesses, homes, schools, libraries, and even airports. The World Wide Web provides instant access to news, reference information, shopping, banking, stock trading, auctions, and travel information and reservations. People routinely use the Internet to take college courses, play games, listen to music, and view videos. Chat rooms and e-mails are now replacing telephones as our favorite means of long-distance communication. The proliferation of computer technology obviously has enhanced our lives in many ways, such as enabling improved productivity and efficiency at work, school, and home. Anyone with access to a computer and modem now has unparalleled recreational and educational opportunities.

Unfortunately, criminals are also using modern technology—to prey on innocent victims. Computers and the Internet have made the predator's job easier. Historically, child predators found their victims in public places where children tend to gather—schoolyards, playgrounds, and shopping malls. Today, with so many children online, the Internet provides predators a new place—cyberspace—to target children for criminal acts. This approach eliminates many of the risks predators face when making contact in person.

The sheer number of young people using computers today makes our concern for them well founded. Recent years have seen a great increase in access to and use of the Internet. By the end of 1998, more than 40 percent of all American homes had computers, and 25 percent had Internet access. This trend is expected to continue. Children and teenagers are one of the fastest growing groups of Internet users. An estimated 10 million kids are online today. By the year 2002, this figure is expected to increase to 45 million, and by 2005 to 77 million.With so many youth online and vulnerable to predators, it is extremely important for parents, law enforcement officials, prosecutors, and victim service providers to know as much as possible about Internet crimes against children so they can prevent victimization and prosecute offenders.

Who Is Vulnerable?

Traditionally, both intrafamilial offenders and strangers have found that young children and teenagers are perfect targets for criminal acts because they are often trusting, naive, curious, adventuresome, and eager for attention and affection. However, the most attractive factor to predators is that children and teenagers historically have not been viewed as credible witnesses. Today, the danger to children is even greater because the Internet provides predators anonymity. Whether the victimization occurs in person or over the Internet, the process is the same—the perpetrator uses information to target a child victim. For example, the predator may initiate an online friendship with a young person, sharing hobbies and interests. This may lead to the exchange of gifts and pictures. Just like the traditional predator who targets children in person, the online predator usually is willing to spend considerable time befriending and grooming a child. The predator wants to build the child's trust, which will allow the predator to get what he or she ultimately wants from the child.

Although no family is immune to the possibility that their child may be exploited and harassed on the Internet, a few factors make some children more vulnerable than others. Older children tend to be at greater risk because they often use the computer unsupervised and are more likely to engage in online discussions of a personal nature. Some victims become unwitting participants as they actively participate in chat rooms, trade e-mail messages, and send pictures online. Troubled or rebellious teens who are seeking emancipation from parental authority can be susceptible to Internet predators. The risk of victimization is greater for emotionally vulnerable youth who may be dealing with issues of sexual identity. These young people may be willing to engage in conversation that is both titillating and exciting but appears innocent and harmless. Unfortunately, Internet interactions that initially appear innocent can gradually lead to sexually explicit conduct

Types of Internet Victimization

Internet crimes are often thought of as victimless. Nothing could be further from the truth. Children and teenagers can and do become victims of Internet crimes. Predators contact teenagers and children over the Internet and victimize them by

— Enticing them through online contact for the purpose of engaging them in sexual acts.

— Using the Internet for the production, manufacture, and distribution of child pornography.

— Using the Internet to expose youth to child pornography and encourage them to exchange pornography.

— Enticing and exploiting children for the purpose of sexual tourism (travel with the intent to engage in sexual behavior) for commercial gain and/or personal gratification.

Unique Characteristics of Cybercrimes

Several characteristics distinguish Internet crimes from other crimes committed against children:

— Physical contact between the child and the perpetrator does not need to occur for a child to become a victim or for a crime to be committed. Innocent pictures or images of children can be digitally transformed into pornographic material and distributed across the Internet without the victims' knowledge.

— The Internet provides a source for repeated, long-term victimization of a child that can last for years, often without the victim's knowledge. Once a child's picture is displayed on the Internet, it can remain there forever. Images can stay on the Internet indefinitely without damage to the quality of the image.

— These crimes transcend jurisdictional boundaries, often involving multiple victims from different communities, states, and countries. The geographic location of a child is not a primary concern for perpetrators who target victims over the Internet. Often, perpetrators travel hundreds of miles to different states and countries to engage in sexual acts with children they met over the Internet. Many of these cases involve local, state, federal, and international law enforcement entities in multiple jurisdictions.

— Many victims of Internet crimes do not disclose their victimization or even realize that they have been victims of a crime. Whereas children who experience physical or sexual abuse may disclose the abuse to a friend, teacher, or parent, many victims of Internet crimes remain anonymous until pictures or images are discovered by law enforcement during an investigation. The presumed anonymity of Internet activities often provides a false sense of security and secrecy for both the perpetrator and the victim.

How Parents Can Reduce the Risks

While children need a certain amount of privacy, they also need parental involvement and supervision in their daily lives. The same general parenting skills that apply to the "real world" also apply while online.

If you have cause for concern about your children's online activities, talk to them. Also seek out the advice and counsel of teachers, librarians, and other Internet and online service users in your area. Open communication with your children, utilization of such computer resources, and getting online yourself will help you obtain the full benefits of these systems and alert you to any potential problem that may occur with their use. If your child tells you about an upsetting person or thing encountered while online, don't blame your child but help him or her avoid problems in the future. Remember — how you respond will determine whether they confide in you the next time they encounter a problem and how they learn to deal with problems on their own.

Beyond these basics, there are some specific things that you should know about the Internet. For instance, did you know that there are web sites and newsgroups that have material that is hateful, is violent, or contains other types of material that parents might consider to be inappropriate for their children? It's possible for children to stumble across this type of material when doing a search using one of the web sites that is specifically designed to help people find information on the Internet. Most of these sites (called "search engines") do not, by default, filter out material that might be inappropriate for children, but some offer a child-safe option and some are designed specifically for use by children.

Also the Internet contains web sites, newsgroups, and other areas designed specifically for adults who wish to post, view, or read sexually explicit material including stories, pictures, and videos. Some of this material is posted on web sites where there is an attempt to verify the user's age and/or a requirement for users to enter a credit card number on the presumption that children do not have access to credit card numbers. Other areas on the Internet make no such effort to control access. Nevertheless, consider monitoring your credit card bills for such charges.

Some online services and ISPs allow parents to limit their children's access to certain services and features such as adult-oriented web sites and "chat" rooms and bulletin boards. There may be an area set aside just for kids where you don't have to worry about them stumbling onto inappropriate material or getting into an unsupervised chat.

At the very least, keep track of any files your children download to the computer, consider sharing an E-mail account with your children to oversee their mail, and consider joining your children when they are in private chat areas.

In addition, there are filtering features built into the popular Internet browsers (the software you use to access the World Wide Web) that empower parents to limit their children's access only to those sites that have been rated appropriate for children. Other useful tools are software programs that block web sites, newsgroups, and chat areas that are known to be inappropriate for children. Most of these programs can be configured by the parent to filter out sites that contain nudity, sexual content, hateful or violent material, or that advocate the use of drugs, tobacco, or alcohol. Some can also be configured to prevent children from revealing information about themselves such as their name, address, or telephone number. You can find a directory of these filtering programs at www.safekids.com/filters.htm.

While technological child-protection tools are worth exploring, they're not a panacea. Regardless of whether you choose to use a filtering program or an Internet rating system, the best way to assure that your children are having positive online experiences is to stay in touch with what they are doing. One way to do this is to spend time with your children while they're online. Have them show you what they do, and ask them to teach you how to use the Internet or online service. You might be surprised at how much you can learn from your kids.

Guidelines for Parents

By taking responsibility for your children's online computer use, parents can greatly minimize any potential risks of being online. Make it a family rule to

— Never give out identifying information — home address, school name, or telephone number — in a public message such as chat or bulletin boards (newsgroup), and be sure you're dealing with someone that both you and your child know and trust before giving out this information via E-mail. Think carefully before revealing any personal information such as age, marital status, or financial information. Do not post photographs of your children on web sites or newsgroups that are available to the public. Consider using a pseudonym, avoid listing your child's name and E-mail address in any public directories and profiles, and find out about your ISP's privacy policies and exercise your options for how your personal information may be used.

— Get to know the Internet and any services your child uses. If you don't know how to log on, get your child to show you. Have your child show you what he or she does online, and become familiar with all the things that you can do online.

— Never allow a child to arrange a face-to-face meeting with another computer user without parental permission. If a meeting is arranged, make the first one in a public place, and be sure to accompany your child.

— Never respond to messages or bulletin board items that are suggestive, obscene, belligerent, threatening, or make you feel uncomfortable. Encourage your children to tell you if they encounter such messages. If you or your child receives a message that is harassing, of a sexual nature, or threatening, forward a copy of the message to your ISP, and ask for their assistance. Instruct your child ***not*** to click on any links that are contained in E-mail from persons they don't know. Such links could lead to sexually explicit or otherwise inappropriate web sites.

— Remember that people online may not be who they seem. Because you can't see or even hear the person it would be easy for someone to misrepresent him- or herself. Thus, someone indicating that "she" is a "12-year-old girl" could in reality be a 40-year-old man.

— Remember that everything you read online may not be true. Any offer that's "too good to be true" probably is. Be very careful about any offers that involve you coming to a meeting, having someone visit your house, or sending money or credit card information.

— Set reasonable rules and guidelines for computer use by your children Discuss these rules and post them near the computer as a reminder. Remember to monitor your children's compliance with these rules, especially when it comes to the amount of time your children spend on the computer. A child's excessive use of online services or the

Internet, especially late at night, may be a clue that there is a potential problem. Remember that personal computers and online services should not be used as electronic babysitters.

— Check out blocking, filtering, and ratings.

— Be sure to make this a family activity. Consider keeping the computer in a family room rather than the child's bedroom. Get to know their "online friends" just as you get to know all of their other friends.

FIREWALL

You can probably guess what a firewall does just from its name. The idea is a simple one, which is why it works so well: A firewall ABSOLUTELY ISOLATES your computer from the Internet using a "wall of code" that inspects each individual "packet" of data as it arrives at either side of the firewall — inbound to or outbound from your computer — to determine whether it should be allowed to pass or be blocked.

A firewall is a super cool idea. This is so true, that someday firewalls will be standard equipment on all PC's. There's no question about it.

In fact, the PC Industry press now reports that the next version of Microsoft Windows, codenamed "Whistler", will include a built-in firewall. However, its exact nature and capabilities are currently unknown. But today, firewalls need to be added where needed — which is pretty much everywhere.

How does a Firewall Work?

All internet communication is accomplished by the exchange of individual "packets" of data. Each packet is transmitted by its source machine toward its destination machine. Packets are the fundamental unit of information flow across the Internet. Even though we refer to "connections" between computers, this "connection" is actually comprised of individual packets travelling between those two "connected" machines. Essentially, they "agree" that they're connected and each machine sends back "acknowledgement packets" to let the sending machine know that the data was received.

In order to reach its destination — whether it's another computer two feet away or two continents distant — every Internet packet must contain a destination address and port number. And, so that the receiving computer knows who sent the packet, every packet must also contain the IP address and a port number of the originating machine. In other words, any packet travelling the net contains — first and foremost — its complete source and destination addresses. As we've seen earlier on this site, an IP address always identifies a single machine on the Internet and the port is associated with a particular service or conversation happening on the machine.

Since the firewall software inspects each and every packet of data as it arrives at your computer — BEFORE it's seen by any other software running within your computer — the firewall has total veto power over your computer's receipt of anything from the Internet.

A TCP/IP port is only "open" on your computer if the first arriving packet which requests the establishment of a connection is answered by your computer. If the arriving packet is simply ignored, that port of your computer will effectively disappear from the Internet. No one and nothing can connect to it!

But the real power of a firewall is derived from its ability to be selective about what it lets through and what it blocks. Since every arriving packet must contain the correct IP address of the sender's machine, (in order for the receiver to send back a receipt acknowledgement) the firewall can be selective about which packets are admitted and which are dropped. It can "filter" the arriving packets based upon any combination of the originating machine's IP address and port and the destination machine's IP address and port.

So, for example, if you were running a web server and needed to allow remote machines to connect to your machine on port 80 (http), the firewall could inspect every arriving packet and only permit connection initiation on your port 80. New connections would be denied on all other ports. Even if your system were to inadvertently pick up a Trojan horse program which opened a Trojan listening port to the outside world, no passing Trojan scanner could detect or know of the Trojan's existence since all attempts to contact the Trojan inside your computer would be blocked by the firewall!

Or suppose that you wish to create a secure "tunnel" across the Internet to allow your home and office computers to share their files without any danger of unauthorized intrusion. Firewall technology makes this possible and relatively simple. You would instruct the firewall running on your office computer to permit connections on the NetBIOS file sharing ports 137-139 only from the IP address of your home computer. The firewall running on your home machine would similarly be instructed to permit connections on ports 137-139 only from your office machine's IP address. Thus, either machine can "see" the other's NetBIOS ports, but no one else on the Internet can see that either machine has established such a secure tunnel across the Net.

But what about you originating your own connections to other machines on the Internet? For example, when you surf the web you need to connect to web servers that might have any IP address. You wouldn't want all those to be blocked just because you want to block everyone from getting into your machine. It turns out that this is easy for a firewall too. Since each end of an Internet connection is always acknowledging the other end's data, every packet that flows between the two machines has a bit set in it called the "ACK" bit. This bit says that the packet is acknowledging the receipt of all previous data. But this means that only the very first packet which initiates a new connection would NOT be acknowledging any previous data from the other machine. In other words, a firewall can easily determine whether an arriving packet is initiating a new connection, or continuing an existing conversation. Packets arriving as part of an established connection would be allowed to pass through the firewall, but packets representing new connection attempts would be discarded. Thus, a firewall can permit the establishment of outbound connections while blocking any new connection attempts from the outside.

Another example of the power of a high-quality firewall is "application level" filtering and response: Most firewalls do pretty much what I've explained above, and this affords tremendous protection. But they don't attempt to "understand" the data in the packets they're admitting or blocking. Their "permit" or "deny" decisions are only based upon the source and destination addresses. But an "application level" firewall involves itself in the actual dialog taking place. For example, we've seen that one of the biggest problems with Microsoft's file and printer sharing is its lack of ability to prevent password crackers from pounding away on a password until it's broken. But an intelligent application level firewall can monitor what's happening on port 139 (where password protection occurs) and step in to completely block an offending remote computer! It can automatically "black list" the originating IP address to completely prevent any and all future access from that outsider.

INDEX